THE ENCYCLOPEDIA OF WEALTH BUILDING FINANCIAL OPPORTUNITIES

MONEY MANUAL NO. 1—**PLANT YOUR DOLLARS IN REAL ESTATE AND WATCH THEM GROW**
The Basics Of Real Estate Investing

MONEY MANUAL NO. 2—**INVESTMENT OPPORTUNITIES OF THE 1980'S**
Wealth Building Strategies In The Stock Market, Gold, Silver, Diamonds...

MONEY MANUAL NO. 3—**SECRETS OF THE MILLIONAIRES**
How The Rich Made It Big

MONEY MANUAL NO. 4—**DYNAMICS OF PERSONAL MONEY MANAGEMENT**
How To Save, Manage, And Multiply Your Money

MONEY MANUAL NO. 5—**THE NEW AGE OF BANKING**
Secrets Of Banking And Borrowing

MONEY MANUAL NO. 6—**HOW TO START MAKING MONEY IN A BUSINESS OF YOUR OWN**
A Guide To Money Making Opportunities

MONEY MANUAL NO. 7—**HOW TO SAVE ON TAXES AND TAKE ALL THE DEDUCTIONS YOU ARE ENTITLED TO**

THE NEW AGE OF BANKING

Secrets of Banking and Borrowing

Published by

George Sterne
Profit Ideas
8361 Vickers St., Suite 304
San Diego, CA 92111

ACKNOWLEDGEMENTS

The publishers wish to express thanks to Bob Rose and Russ von Hoelscher for their contributions of research and writing to this book.

THE NEW AGE OF BANKING

Secrets of Banking and Borrowing

Table of Contents

Chapter One

THE NEW AGE OF BANKING

Competition for your dollar has never been as fierce as it is today. Financial institutions want you as a customer, particularly as a saver. Since you and your "business" are in such great demand, it is wise to shop around for the best deals and best financial institutions with which to deal.

REASONS FOR SAVINGS

Most thrifty people have a savings account with some sort of institution, whether it be a bank, savings and loan, insurance, credit union, etc. Savings acts as an ace in the hole for whatever emergencies arise, such as medical expenses, auto repairs, fixing sudden leaks in plumbing, and countless other unexpected expenses. There is also the possibility the family bread winner might suddenly lose his job, and a nice nest egg can help tide the troubled times over until he is able to find another job.

With job security, people like to save money for short-term projects such as the family vacation, a down payment on a second car, new carpeting in the home, Christmas, and others. Again, there are long-range projects such as a child to be married, college funds, retirement, and so on. Some people even have a savings account simply as a credit reference for taking out loans.

Whatever the reason for saving, it is a good idea to have some sort of savings. Unfortunately, too many people stick their money in an institution with the idea that their money is earning interest, and left there long enough, they will accumulate a tidy sum. The truth of the matter is, they are losing more dollars than can be seen on the surface.

LOSING MONEY IN SAVINGS

Many people are blind to the fact that even though their savings may be earning the highest interest rates, they are actually losing money every year.

The cost of whatever you save for goes up because of inflation. For instance, if you were saving $6,000 over a period of five years, for a fishing boat, at the end of your goal you are apt to find, through inflation, the same boat costs twice as much as the original price. In other words, you have underestimated your original goal.

At the same time inflation eats up your dollars, the actual value of the dollars you save goes down. If inflation is 10% and you are getting 5% interest, you are going backwards!

Then there are taxes that chew up incomes. Even the interest on your savings are subject to taxation.

Under the impression that your savings are drawing maximum interest, it is possible to lose hundreds of dollars on those savings. While most banks advertise the same interest rates, what they actually pay can make a difference of hundreds of dollars. The difference is in the method of computing interest rates.

COMPOUND INTEREST

The method by which banks compute interest, or compounding interest, to use bank terminology, determines the actual dollar amount your savings will earn. To illustrate this point: three banks advertise 5¼% on a regular passbook savings of $1,000.

Bank X computes interest once a year and pays $52.50 in interest. Bank Y computes interest quarterly, paying you $53.69 at the end of the year. Bank Z compounds interest daily and you obtain $53.90 at the end of the year.

One might consider that a paltry sum and ask is it really worth the trouble? Yes, indeed! The difference in this illustration was based on a $1,000 account. When adding to the money in the account, the interest will increase.

Let's face it—saving money to earn money is a business, just like selling cars. If a customer likes a special car, the salesman might persuade the customer to buy the same with an added option, like a tape deck for a couple hundred dollars in commission which adds up at the end of the month.

The same thing applies to savings. At the end of the second year, the savings in Bank X will have earned interest on $1,052.50, while Bank Z is compounding interest on $1,053.90. Remember Bank Z is compounding interest daily. As time goes by, the difference turns to tens of dollars, and eventually hundreds.

THE BALANCE BEING PAID ON

How often a bank pays interest is only one consideration. What balance they pay on is something else again and can mean a considerable amount. Look at the difference of what you get from our three banks on what balance they pay.

The banks advertise 5¼% a year compounded simiannually. You deposit $1,000 every month for six months, withdrawing none.

Bank X pays on the minimum balance, which was $1,000. You earn $26.25. (A lot of banks still do it this way.) Bank Y pays on the *average* balance, which is $3,000. You earn $78.75. (Most banks compute in this method.) Bank Z pays the *maximum* balance of $6,000. You earn $157.50. However, very few banks offer this unless they are new banks offering a limited service such as this to attract customers.

Here is another consideration. Banks Y and Z pay 5¼% a year compounded quarterly. Both pay on the minimum balance. You deposit $1,000 a month for three months.

Bank Y computes on the quarter and you earn $13.12 on the minimum balance of $1,000. Bank Z computes the balance every month giving you $16.25 for the quarter. What happens is that when Bank Z computes the balance every month, it averages the minimum each month and pays you on the quarter. But when they compute the balance every month, you don't collect interest on the interest until the next quarter.

In all cases, it was not how much interest the bank paid,

but how they computed it that makes the difference in how much you actually earned.

CHOOSE THE RIGHT ONE FOR YOU

When choosing your savings institution, you want to keep in mind these things:

1. How much interest they pay.
2. How often interest is computed.
3. What balance they pay on.
4. The method of computation.

Plan to visit several institutions. Take a calculator with you.

DEPOSITING AND WITHDRAWING

Another thing to watch for is how you deposit and withdraw money. *When* you deposit makes a difference on how soon you will start earning interest. For example, if a bank computes second quarter interest in June, and you made the deposit in May, your money may not start earning interest until the third quarter.

If you withdraw your savings in May, you will not earn interest for that quarter since you took out the money too soon.

Sometimes a bank will insist on you making a deposit slip and withdrawal slip every time you cash a check. In other words, you are depositing money into your savings and then withdrawing it again.

What is actually happening, the new money is being posted to your account; the money you withdraw is actually the oldest money in the account. Therefore, you are losing interest on the money that has been in the account, the money that has the greatest earning potential. Over an extended period of time you would find a total loss of interest in the account.

Most banks, however, offer check cashing as a free service to their customers. But if you are the type who dips into your savings at the end of the month, remember that every time you withdraw money from savings, you are taking out the oldest money in the account.

To beat that, consider having two savings accounts: one passbook account from which you can withdraw freely and a timed savings from which you cannot withdraw for a period without losing interest.

TYPES OF SAVINGS ACCOUNTS

While it is agreed that everyone should have some type of savings account, what type of savings to have is hard to choose because there are as many different types of savings accounts as there are fish in the sea. What you choose should depend on the reason you save and how soon you expect to use the savings.

Most banks have five or more different types of accounts. Most have a passbook account which requires a small minimum balance—$5.00 or $10.00—and offers complete flexibility as to when and the amount of money that can be deposited or withdrawn.

16

Certificates of deposit are timed accounts. In other words, the money deposited must be left in for a minimum period in order to accumulate the highest interest rate. The minimum time is called the maturity date and after that funds may be withdrawn without penalty. Maturity times range from as little as three months to 10 years.

Savings may be in the form of Stocks and Bonds, insurance, and other investments. One of the best institutions to save in is a Credit Union. When you open an account, you are a shareholder in the Union. Not only do your savings earn higher interest rates than banks, you also receive a share of the dividends. The drawback is that membership is restricted, usually to certain organizations and companies.

Most institutions have three types of savings accounts; Individual, Joint, and Revocable Trust accounts.

INSURED SAVINGS

A big advantage to saving in a commercial institution is that your savings are insured up to $100,000 by the Federal Savings and Loan Insurance Corporation. If your bank goes broke, you will still get your $100,000 back if you had that much in savings.

With the right combination of individual, joint, and trust accounts, a small family can maintain a large amount of insured savings. For a family of four, insured savings can be up to $1,400,000. See the example on next page.

Individual Accounts

Husband. $100,000
Wife $100,000
Child one $100,000
Child two $100,000

Joint Accounts

Husband and wife. $100,000
Husband and child one. $100,000
Wife and child two $100,000
Child one and two. $100,000

Revocable Trust

Husband as trustee for wife $100,000
Wife as trustee for husband $100,000
Husband and child one. $100,000
Wife as trustee for child one $100,000
Husband as trustee child two $100,000
Wife as trustee for child two $100,000

The grand total is $1,400,000.

The total insured figure can be increased when grand-parents set up accounts for grandchildren.

When you get down to it, the larger the family, the larger the insured savings possible.

SAVINGS AT NEW INSTITUTIONS

That new bank on the corner can be a goldmine in savings and loans if you play your cards right. While the people who work there have had prior experience in banking, the bank itself will relax whatever restrictions they can to attract new customers. Loan restrictions are relaxed to obtain customers and high-interest savings plans are offered to a limited number until the business gets rolling.

Clear thinking and asking questions will help you obtain an excellent savings plan with high returns on your money.

A case in point; a young college couple received a sizable inheritance. After taxes, they had $1,000,000. The husband, a business major, took the million to a new bank and offered to deposit it in a savings plan without withdrawing a dime for 10 years, provided the bank mailed monthly interest to his residence. The bank agreed, offering a 10% annual interest. The couple received about $6,000 a month from the bank each month, which they used for living expenses. They both completed college and borrowed money from the same bank to start their own business.

But imagine having to make a living on a mere $6,000 a month!

NOTES

NOTES

Chapter Two

HOW TO BORROW MONEY

WHY BORROW?

Few Americans ever go through life without having to borrow money. Borrowing is a way of life in this country and actually increases our standard of living.

Businesses today have to borrow money constantly to stay in business. Rarely has anyone ever had enough money to start a new business and keep it going without ever having to borrow more or depend on credit.

There are few customers who have never had to rely on borrowing money or credit to make it through life. Those who don't are either independently wealthy and can pay for EVERYTHING in cash, or are so poor that they never can buy anything anyway.

There are so many ways of borrowing money that it would take volumes of books to write about them all. Here in Chapter two we'll discuss consumer loans and touch on the best known methods of obtaining a loan. While Chapter two will not cover business loans, we will mention many techniques which can also be used in business.

When you, the consumer, borrow money, you should approach it with a business-like attitude. Who, how, what, where, when, and why you borrow can make the difference between prosperity and bankruptcy. You want to borrow as much as you need for as long as you can at the least possible cost. Banks and lending institutions make it a business lending you money. In return, you should treat borrowing as a business matter, no matter what the reason you borrow.

When you borrow, you are actually buying money to buy goods and services you may not otherwise be able to afford. This applies to all types of consumer credit, whether it be a direct loan, a charge card, or paying for goods in installments. You pay for the money you borrow, even if you never see the money.

Presenting a charge card in payment for a dinner at a fancy restaurant merely guarantees the bill will be paid. The charge card company sends the restaurant the money and you in turn pay the card company—usually more than the actual dinner bill.

At the end of the month, you get a bill for $120 for something you bought that only cost $100. You of course can pay it back in easy monthly installments, but the idea of paying a few extra dollars more makes you wonder if it is all really worth it.

Ask yourself if you would have been able to afford it without credit. Does it really put a bind on your budget to pay out a few dollars a month? Could life be more pleasant without the use of credit?

If the answer to any of these questions is *yes,* you may be in serious financial trouble. You may be overspending as a direct result of credit. Another loan will not help.

By no means should borrowing money, nor the use of credit, be discouraged. When not abused, it helps us increase our standard of living. The credit-wise man can drive a new car every year. The fool and the penny pincher who buys everything with cash may walk for a long time.

Before we get into the how and where to borrow money, let's consider a few tips that will help us in making the right decision. It would be impossible for us to tell you the best place to go since everyone's needs are different. It is up to you to do the leg work, but with these tips, you should be able to find the right place for you.

INTEREST

Interest is the amount of money you have to pay on the amount you borrow. In most instances, it is an annual charge you have to pay on the unpaid balance. If you pay $110 on a $100 loan, the $10 is the interest at a rate of 10%.

Suppose you borrow $1,000 for one year at 12% interest, in monthly installments. Each month you are paying 1% interest on the unpaid balance. If you pay $100 for the first payment, $90 actually goes toward the principle of $1,000, and the other $10 pays for the interest. Each month you pay, the amount going toward the interest becomes smaller.

Some lending institutions will add the 12% to the $1,000, then divide the total amount by the number of months you pay back. In this case it is 12 months, giving a total of $1,120 at $93.33 per month.

So which is cheaper? The first one by approximately

$30,00. Not only would your monthly payments be less, if you were to pay a few extra dollars each month, the difference would be greater still. Whenever dealing with money, it is wise to brush up on your math.

FINANCE CHARGES

Now you are all set to get a loan from the company who charges interest on the unpaid balance, right? Maybe. One of the most important factors to consider is finance charges.

A finance charge is the extra amount loan institutions tack on to the total amount you owe to pay for the cost of processing your loan. Just how much that charge is depends on the institution, how much you are borrowing, and how long you are going to take to pay it back. Institutions use this extra money to defray the cost of processing your loan, checking your credit background, giving the payment books or sending you bills, and sending you late notices, if any.

The ways of imposing and disguising finance charges are many, and some institutions are very clever at this. Not much can be done about this because if the government legislated true interest rates on loans, the lending of money would stop altogether, because no one would be able to afford to lend you money.

A few of the better institutions have a standard finance charge depending on the length of time you take out the loan. It costs about the same to process any loan whether it be $100 or $100,000. How many times they send you a bill will add to the cost.

Shop around when you need a loan. Tell the loan officer you have good credit and want to take out a loan and that you want to know what the finance charge is and what it is paying for. If they really want to do business with you, they'll give you the figures. Be sure to get them in writing.

When you've completed your search and made your calculation, you may find the company with the straight annual interest charge is cheaper because they charge you less in finance charges than the company that has you pay interest on the unpaid balance.

BORROWING MONEY
WITH OVERDRAFT CHECKING

Here we depart from standard banking information to give our readers new insights into alternative means of borrowing money. The overdraft checking account program is a shining example of liberal American banking practices. It is very easy to obtain a loan . . . so easy, in fact, that some folks get overextended and into financial hot water quickly. With competition between banks at an all time high, look for more and more financial institutions to offer overdraft checking.

More and more businessmen and investors can use overdraft checking accounts for instant capital to start a new business, expand a present business, or take advantage of an excellent investing opportunity. Raising *fast cash* is often absolutely essential to taking advantage of a super deal. The normal channels of applying for loans at savings and loan associations and banks can be too time-consuming, bureaucratic, and unproductive.

OVERDRAFT CHECKING AT WORK

The overdraft checking account is simply a *line of credit* made available by your regular checking account. Some banks offer separate special accounts for a credit line, but in most cases, regular checking accounts are used. With this modern checking account, an overdrawn account no longer means you have a "bounced" check and a "bad boy" image. Instead, the bank simply pays the would-be *rubber check* and lends you the overdrawn amount at a specified daily interest rate until you bring your account back to a state of balance.

The special accounts come under many headings: ready-cash reserve, sure reserve, guaranteed balance, check-o-draft, guaranteed reserve, etc.

Financial institutions who offer this valuable form of borrowing are now found in almost all large cities and most small towns, nationwide.

HOW MUCH CAN YOU BORROW?

On each individual account, the amount you will be able to borrow varies from area to area and bank to bank. The 1981 range is from $1,000 to $30,000. With inflation constantly on an upward spiral, you can expect limits to reach $50,000 and higher in the not-too-distant future. Keep in mind, this is *signature-only borrowing.* Your signature on a small piece of paper gets you an instant loan!

MORE BENEFITS OF OVERDRAFT CHECKING

In addition to obtain quick money via the instant loan,

there are many other benefits of using the very legal and very helpful (in many cases) overdraft checking system. It is a very convenient method to borrow money without even leaving your own home or office. It is probably the easiest method to obtain a loan. It can be used as an all-purpose loan. Most banks and savings and loan associations have all sorts of different rules you must meet to get different types of loans. By using the overdraft checking method, you decide how to use the money!. . . for business, investments, a new car, color TV, or whatever! Privacy is also guaranteed. Even the financial institution need not know how or where the money is to be used. Add to all these other positive factors, low stable interest rates that allow you to gain a further inflation hedge. You pay back today's loan with tomorrow's dollars, which likely will be of lesser value, even after deducting interest. Most financial institutions are charging 12% on overdraft checking loans. That's less than the major charge cards and other financial lending companies.

You will have to shop around for the lowest rates, but even if you pay 12%-13% interest, you can be the winner providing you use the checking loan to your maximum benefit. Color TV's, cars, and vacations are fine, but only if you can afford them. I suggest a person only use overdraft checking to take advantage of an outstanding investment or business opportunity. This is a powerful leverage tool in the hands of a true entrepreneur.

WHAT THEY LOOK FOR WHEN YOU APPLY FOR A LOAN

Certainly no one is going to willingly lend you money without the assurance that you will pay it back. Your word of honor is not going to be enough, since there are too many people who are not as honest as you.

Most institutions will have you fill out a loan application asking you where you work, how much income you have, credit references, personal references, where you live, and countless other items that may seem meaningless to you.

The information they ask is what they use to check your credibility. Your credibility adds up to three things that sometimes overlap: your character, ability to repay, and willingness to repay.

CHARACTER

Are you honest and sincere? Of course you are. But the lending institutions don't know that. So they check out the references you've listed on your application.

The first thing they look at is your job. What kind of worker are you? How's your future with the company? Are you well liked? What was your last job? Why did you leave it? The questions are endless and they check out each and every one.

Your job or profession may be an important indicator of your character. Hopping around from one job to another indicates employment instability. The longer you have been on your current job the better your chances for loan approval. What your boss says makes a difference too. If he says you are a good worker and he's thinking of putting you in for a promotion, the better for you. If you and your boss don't get along too well, but your job is secure by higher-ups, it might be wise to put their name on the application instead of your immediate supervisor.

The most important aspect of your character is your credit rating. Just about everything you have ever bought on credit is recorded at a credit bureau. The lending institution simply calls them and asks for a rating. Have you missed any payments? Have you had any injunctions against you to make payments? Have you skipped out on any payments? Have you filed bankruptcy? How many open accounts do you have now? If you have missed putting something on the application, the company will ask you about it later.

Honesty is the best policy in determining your character. If you have had some credit problems, past or present, let the loan officer know about it in advance. Loans have been granted to bad credit risks simply because the applicant was incredibly honest in filling out the application and told the loan officer about some past problems. Not only may your loan be granted, but they may help you solve your credit problems with counseling and good sound advice. If they personally can't grant you the loan, they will guide you to someone who can. All because you didn't try to hide anything from the loan officer.

ABILITY TO REPAY

The first place lending institutions look to find out your ability to repay is your job. They want to know your job is stable and that you are getting paid what you claim. In many cases, they make loans to help people through a temporary layoff when they know they'll get their job back. If you lose your job for some reason, and need money to help you along

30

until you can find another, they may grant the loan if they know you can easily find another job.

How much you earn is important. More than that, how much you *spend* is taken into consideration. If your take home pay is $30,000 a year, you might be considered a bad risk if your total expenditures are $20,000.

Add together all your monthly expenditures such as rent or mortgage, auto payments, credit card payments, medical bills, utilities, and anything else you are making time payments on. (For some reason, most institutions don't take monthly food expense into consideration.) Subtract that figure from your total takehome pay. (Include salary, alimony, and any other cash you receive.) If your outgo is greater than 55% of your income you may have trouble getting a loan unless it is a bill consolidation that will bring you under the 55% mark.

Loan institutions agree, as a rule of thumb, that you should have 45% of your income left over each month to pay for gas, food, entertainment, etc. Anything less than 45% indicates you are spending too much and are a bad risk. It could hamper your ability to pay. This goes even if you take home $100,000 a month and have expenditures totalling $60,000. If you lost your job or took a cut in pay, you would be hard pressed to make your payments.

The 45% rule is a safety valve in determining your ability to pay. It is also a good budgeting rule for the home. Don't let your expenditures go over 55%. Put some money in savings instead of buying something else.

Your credit rating and what you own go hand in hand in determining your ability to pay. If you have successfully paid off some of your bills, you now own what you have been paying for such as furniture, auto, home, etc. Not only have you established your rating as good, you also have something you can use as collateral. A good credit rating automatically proves you manage your finances well.

WILLINGNESS TO REPAY

The hardest thing for a loan institution to discover, and for you to prove, is your willingness to repay a loan. Willingness alone can and will make the difference on a yes or no on your loan application, even if your credit rating is bad, and your ability to repay is questionable.

Your character trait of honesty is an important factor in determining your willingness to repay. So is your collateral. For instance, are you willing to put up your house as collateral, knowing that if you default you might be sleeping in an alley? Many people prize their possessions more than they do money. Lenders know this. If you offer your most prized possession as collateral on a loan, you are, in effect, telling your lender, "Hey, I don't want to lose my house, so you know I'll pay you back as we agreed."

This works especially if you offer more collateral than you are asking for in the loan.

Sometimes it works in reverse.

A ventriloquist once offered his two dummies as collateral for a $1,200 loan. Though the dummies were worth less than half that amount, they represented his sole means of support. The company manager was impressed by his willingness to repay the loan and not only granted it, he also gave the ventriloquist some job leads.

THINK TAXES WHEN YOU BORROW

Whenever you borrow money, keep in mind the tax angle. The interest you pay on a loan or any credit for that matter is deductible on your income tax. That you can make a bundle on your income tax by borrowing money is true. Because of the tax angle alone, many people borrow money for investments and get rich doing it.

CUTTING LOAN COSTS

Before you apply for a loan, sit down and figure out how much you need and the maximum amount you can safely pay out each month. Make sure that the amount you can pay each month has a 10% fudge factor that will cover the cost of the loan.

Now look again at the amount you want to borrow. If it is a small sum, you can expect to pay a high interest rate. Normally, the greater the amount you wish to borrow, the less the interest rate will be. The longer the time you borrow for will also bring down the interest rate. If you obtain a broker's manual for your state, a quick glance will tell you what the interest rate is on the length of time for the amount you borrow.

Suppose you wanted to borrow $5,000 for a down payment on a motor home and your payments are $150 a month for 36 months. The interest rate is, say, 15%.

You figure you can safely pay back at a rate of $200 per month for 30 months. The interest rate might probably be 16% because of the shorter time period you take out the loan. But if you were to borrow $6,500 for 36 months, your interest might be only 14% with payments of $200 per month.

With these three options open to you, you need only figure out the total cost of the loan to find the best option.

There is another option open to you. You can borrow the $5,000 for 36 months. Instead of paying $150, go ahead and pay the $200. In states where interest rates are regulated, finance companies cannot charge you the extra interest simply because you pay off your loan sooner. In effect you are cutting down your actual interest rates. This works especially well when interest is paid on the unpaid balance. If you sat down and figured it out, you would actually be paying less than 12% interest.

Another method of cutting costs is the super short term loan. If you borrowed $1,000 for 1 year at 12% interst and paid it all back in a week, it would cost you less than a dollar interest. You may still have to pay the finance charge, but the money you save in interest would be worth it. Be sure the contract you sign doesn't have a penalty clause for paying off early.

DETERMINING YOUR CREDIT WORTH

How much you are worth can tell you how much you can borrow. The best way to determine this is to add together your total assets and subtract your total liabilities. Everything you own is an asset. Things you are still paying for are assets if you subtract the amount you owe from the current value. Your monthly paycheck is an asset too.

If your current net worth is $25,000, you can probably borrow as much as $100,000 depending on what you are buying, how long you want the money and your ability to repay. If you have a $100,000 net worth, you may be able to borrow $400,000 or more.

Believe it or not, some institutions consider your debts an asset (providing they are not excessive) if you have an excellent credit rating.

If you are buying something which decreases in value each year (i.e., a car) then you should have 10% to 20% on hand as a down payment. Since the item decreases in value and you have paid the down, the down payment is considered equity on which they can collect if you default on payments.

On the other hand, items which increase in value, such as antiques and property, often require little or no down payment. A case in point is the gentleman who put $2,000 down on an eight-unit apartment complex that cost $120,000. The bank was happy to make the loan since the value of apartment complexes was skyrocketing.

I.O.U.'S

If you get an I.O.U., *get it back as soon as you have paid it off!* If you leave it for the creditor to destroy, you might find a letter from a collection agency a few months later. Avoid I.O.U.'s if at all possible.

WATCH OUT FOR THE LOAN SHARKS

As easy as it is to get loans from honest loan companies, some folks still get caught by crafty loan sharks. The results can be disastrous and every effort should be made to avoid them, and get them off the streets.

Here are some tricks they use to trap you:

1. They ask for your receipt for more money than they actually lend you.

2. Ask you to pay off in a very short time.

3. Ask for your signature on a blank note which you will probably never get back.

4. Forget to give you receipts.

5. Want to buy your salary.

6. Ask you for enormous collateral.

7. Are hard to find when you make a payment.

8. Act tough once you've signed.

9. Avoid discussing interest rates.

10. Charge you astronomically high interest.

Should you or anyone you know get hooked by one of these characters, or run into any one of the above situations, contact your attorney and/or the police. More than your money is at stake. Most loan sharks are hardened criminals who will not hesitate to commit violence. They are hard to identify. That nice gentleman who runs the flower shop on the corner might be a loan shark with a police record a mile long. Your only clue will be what he says or neglects to say in discussing a loan.

NOTES

NOTES

Chapter Three

WHERE TO BORROW MONEY

Here are some of the institutions that have money available for loans. Both the advantages and disadvantages of each lending agency will be discussed.

CREDIT UNIONS

If you belong to a credit union, it is an excellent place to obtain a loan. First of all you are a member of the union and they know you. Their cost of processing a loan is much less than almost anywhere else. Once you have established your credit rating with the union they will keep a tally of how much you can borrow on your signature. The more often you borrow money and pay it off, the greater the amount they will lend you on your signature. Secondly, because it is a non-profit organization, their interest rates are lower then banks. Federal regulations keep their interest rates below banks. Thirdly, they are excellent for small loans.

A disadvantage is that you must be a member. If the company you work for does not have a credit union, you may not be able to get into one. Credit Unions are made up of members with a common interest in mind, such as trade unions, large groups of people working in one place, social organizations, and many other types of groups of people who have drawn together to establish a Credit Union. When you have met the organizational requirements for membership, then you must buy a certain amount of shares in the union which is called a savings share. The minimum depends on the credit union and may range from $10 to $100. These savings shares earn interest higher than is offered at banks and you will also collect dividends as well as interest.

Another disadvantage is that they do not make large loans with long term to businesses, to finance homes, or real estate, etc. However, current legislation is in the mills at Congress to allow credit unions to make such loans.

BANKS

Banks offer the most complete service for loans. Their maximum interest rates are regulated by federal law. The maximum amount you can borrow depends on how much you need and your ability to repay.

Because of the costs involved in processing loans, banks do not like to make small loans with short terms, less than $2,000. If they do, it is merely a service for regular customers who have both savings and checking accounts. In some banks, they will allow you to write a check for more than is in your account as an alternative to small loans. Most banks have turned to issuing credit cards instead of making small loans.

However, be sure to give full consideration to the unique *checking account overdraft* plan that was fully outlined in the previous chapter. It may be the best loan vehicle you can get from your banker.

SAVINGS AND LOAN ASSOCIATION

Although quite similar to banks, savings and loan associations do not usually have checking accounts. Some companies do not even cash checks except for their regular customers. Their primary purpose for existence is in their name—savings and loans. Their interest rates on loans are much the same as banks and sometimes are slightly lower. Like banks, they do not like to make small loans, but they do make them. One of the best programs they have for small loans is a savings account loan where you may borrow up to 90% of the amount you have in your savings. You have to pay an interest rate of only 2% above the interest you are receiving from your savings. For instance, if your savings are drawing 5½% interest, you would pay only 7½% interest on your loan. This is far below what you might pay elsewhere and is excellent for financing small purchases. The big advantage to this program is that your savings remain intact, even though you may not be able to withdraw them.

FINANCE COMPANIES

By far, the quickest and easiest place to obtain a loan is from a finance company, which are sometimes called consumer credit companies. They will make loans from $100 to $100,000, depending on the company. It is because of these companies that illegal lending practices and loan sharks have almost disappeared. Their advantage is that you may use almost any reason to borrow, they have relaxed lending restrictions and you get the loan in a day if necessary.

Their big disadvantage is their high interest rates, as well as sometimes hefty finance charges. In most areas, finance companies interest rates are controlled by state governments. Very few of these companies offer savings accounts.

Almost all finance companies either own, or are part of a

massive corporation such as insurance companies and many corporate businesses. With such financial backing, these companies are able to take a risk in making small loans. Many young men and women have established their credit ratings with these companies, and many people in serious financial trouble have gotten out of debt with their help.

LIFE INSURANCE COMPANIES

This is the number one source for loans in the nation. Generally, you can borrow up to 95% of the cash surrender value of your policy. Every year the cash value goes up, the amount you can borrow increases. The interest rate varies between 4% and 6%, depending on the company. Interest rates are usually specified on the policy. It is simple to get a life insurance loan. All you have to do is contact your agent. The agent will give you a form to fill out and you get money within a few days. No hassle, no credit checks, and almost never a denial. The interest you pay is a flat rate with no extras and no hidden charges. Generally, you are not held to a specific time for repayment. The disadvantage is that you might be lulled into maintaining the loan indefinitely, which means you will continue paying interest which will make the cost of the loan high. Another disadvantage is that the amount of the loan decreases the amount of protection your policy offers.

PRIVATE INVESTMENT COMPANIES

Generally these companies are groups of people who put their money together to make loans. Such a company might be a group of doctors investing their money to offset the high cost of malpractice insurance. Most of these companies make business loans. You need only give a good reason for the loan and show that you can pay it back. Depending on the company, you may pay interest rates from 2% to 25% annually. The loans they make may range from $500 to $5 million.

One disadvantage is that they employ brokers to handle their money. The brokers require a deposit, usually about 10%, to offset the cost of setting up and handling the loan. Out of this deposit the broker also takes his fee and you may or may not get some or all of the deposit back. If the loan does not go through, you will usually get all your deposit back.

PARENTS, RELATIVES, AND FRIENDS

Parents, relatives, and friends could be your easiest source for a low cost, or no cost loan, assuming, of course, they have money available and are willing to help. Your interest might be none at all or very little. It is recommended, however, that you offer to pay some interest. This will help your family and friends understand you are not sponging off their generosity, and you are sincere.

The embarrassment of having to ask friends and relatives for a loan could be considered a disadvantage. Also, the lack of pressure to make you repay may make you lazy. You could have that debt hanging over you longer than necessary. Personal relationships may impair your judgement and the amount you borrow may be too large or too small. There is also the possibility of strained relationships and quarreling if you are slow in repaying the loan.

The best way to handle a loan between you and your

friends and relatives is to set it up through a bank. You make regular installment payments directly through a bank in a business-like manner without bothering your creditor. If there is some difficulty, you can talk to the bank about it. Interest can still be waived.

NOTES

NOTES

Chapter Four

THE PROS AND CONS OF SAVING MONEY

When the average person thinks about savings, he or she thinks about money sitting safely in a bank or savings and loan, while earning interest. While American banks and savings and loan associations remain more or less stable, they are generally unable to protect your money against skyrocketing inflation. It is high time the prudent investor, speculator, or entrepreneur stops thinking about his savings account as an absolute proposition to protect hard-earned capital. Savings accounts which earn 5% to 7% interest are nothing more than low risk, low yield conservative investments, and if you end up losing purchasing power because inflation is greater than interest, one could even say, they are not very conservative, just a slow method to watch your dollars erode. To counterattack conventional savings account plans, we must use dynamic 1980's financial tactics and techniques.

GRACE PERIODS AND BONUS DAYS

Let's leave the 5% to 7% interest returns to wealthy little old ladies who inherited much wealth, but who do not wish to risk a dime to improve upon it. You and I can't make out with the small pittance our local bank doles out on typical savings. The key to making some real money, up to a 20% return on a standard savings account is through shrewd use of the bonus days and grace periods offered by many savings and loan associations. The ceiling on regular passbook savings accounts is currently 5¾%. You can do better (but not much better) with time deposit savings, but you also will inherit more restrictions. In order to attract savings accounts

48

from John Q. Public, many S & L's and banks have offered *free gifts* and other *goodies* in the hope folks would bring them more money. When the competition in "free stuff" became hot and heavy, some institutions sweetened the come-on by offering "bonus days" or "grace periods" as a savings inducement. Now a bank or S & L customer could deposit his or her savings on the ninth or tenth of a given month and earn interest from the first. Some S & L's even went so far as to offer 15 and 20-day "bonus days." If you deposited by the 15th or 20th, you earned interest from the first of the month.

Now let's look at ways we could be earning much more interest than the savings and loan association or bank originally intended. To take advantage of these "bonus days" or "grace periods," you would have to open two separate accounts at two different savings institutions. One will pay interest from the day of deposit to the day of withdrawal. The other must be a savings account with 10 or more grace days at the start of month. Between the first and tenth of the month you place a sum of money, let's use $5,000. for this example, in the first bank or savings and loan that pays daily interest. On the tenth of the month, you withdraw your $5,000 plus earned interest from this institution and deposit it in the second S & L or bank which gives 10 grace days. Since you dropped off your money by the tenth, you earn interest from the first. What you have now accomplished is *double interest* for the first 10 days of the month. This entirely legal practice can increase your interest money received by 25% monthly! Even if you can't find a S & L that offers interest on a monthly basis in your area, it is very easy to locate many financial institutions that pay quarterly interest. While still profitable, quarterly interest payments using this plan will be much less than applying this little-known tactic on a monthly basis.

I think we should now mention the drawbacks of this scheme. Since this plan came into wide use in the late 1970's by insiders, many savings and loan associations have stopped offering "bonus days" and "grace periods." Also, some institutions that still make them available will not tolerate regular deposits and withdrawals. When it becomes apparent what you are up to, they may choose to close your account— *quickly*.

We feel the short-range profits of this scheme can be attractive, but are skeptical of the long-range repeat profit picture.

USING THE "FLOAT METHOD"

Another legal scheme that has become popular in the late 1970's-early 1980's is taking advantage of the "Float"—the time it takes your check to clear the Federal Reserve banking system. This is done through the *transfer draft* which is the type of check which allows the transfer of your savings from one S & L to another. This transfer draft can be mailed with your savings passbook to another S & L for deposit. Since you can expect your deposit to start earning interest from the first day received, even though the transfer draft is being sent for collection, you thus earn interest on both accounts. This can really build interest profits, since the transfer will often take up to three weeks to clear. Again, we have an interesting interest-building gimmick that can run up short-range savings profit. For the long pull, we would again be skeptical.

COMMERCIAL BANKS

Commercial banks are not the best banks for consumers

who want to save. Regulation Q imposes the lowest ceiling on interest rates of all the financial and savings institutions in the U.S. Most commercial banks only pay about 5-5½% on their regular savings accounts.

SAVINGS AND LOAN ASSOCIATIONS

Savings and loan companies have a higher ceiling on interest rates they pay on regular savings accounts. Some state S & L's, in fact, are now paying 6% a year, compounded daily, giving an effective annual yield of 6.18% (and progressively higher with each year). These accounts are highly liquid (you can withdraw your money at any time, although most S & L's reserve the right to restrict withdrawal until after 30 days), insured up to $40,000 by the state government, and close to home. If you're unable to join a local credit union (discussed below), then a savings account at an S & L is probably your best deal.

CREDIT UNIONS

We have discussed credit unions before in talking about borrowing money. They also have many virtues when it comes to saving money. In fact, you can probably earn more money at your local credit union than anywhere else. They have the least restrictions on what interest they can pay to their account holders. According to credit union laws, interest is actually *dividends* and customers are *shareholders*. Earnings are determined by the credit union's directors, and although most credit unions are now paying about 6% a year in dividend return, some are paying much higher rates on restricted accounts.

In New York City, for example, the Melrose Credit Union offers its 5,500 members a fantastic 9% interest on its unrestricted savings deposits! The earnings rate fluctuates each year, though, so this 9% figure may not hold. The rates also apply on a minimum quarterly balance. The savings accounts are insured up to $40,000 by the federal government. To join the Melrose Credit Union, you pay a nominal entrance fee and make a minimum $25 deposit. The credit union is 57 years old. It offers many other advantages in terms of low-cost personal and auto loans, et cetera.

As stated earlier, it's becoming quite easy to join a credit union in your own home town. So even though you may not work for the federal government or a large corporation, which usually have credit unions of their own, it may be possible to join an "independent" credit union in the city. In the Washington, D.C., metropolitan area, for example, there are some 300 credit unions, many of which are independent and essentially open to the public (such as the Greenbelt Federal Credit Union or the Washington Area Feminist Credit Union). According to the D.C. League of Credit Unions, there are 1.2 million area residents who could, but have not yet, become members! Some Washington credit unions are now paying 7% on unrestricted savings accounts.

COMPETING INVESTMENTS

As we stated at the beginning of this chapter, your savings are in direct competition with other forms of investments, whether in higher or lower risk and return. These investments might include the stock market, stock options, bonds, money market funds, tax-free municipal bonds, the commodity futures market, commodity options, numismatic coins, real estate, art and antiques, gold and silver, foreign currencies, and old cars. There are hundreds of different places to put your money these days, to be pondered with an eye toward beating the ravages of inflation.

SAVINGS BONDS, SERIES E AND H

One form of competing investment for your savings might be series E and H savings bonds issued by the federal government. *These savings bonds are poor investments in today's inflationary climate and should be avoided.* The government has tried to make these savings bond plans appeal to citizens by making special arrangements for automatic payroll deduction to buy series E bonds—but don't take the bait!

These bonds have serious defects. Series E bonds, for example, cannot be transferred, sold, or used as collateral (unlike treasury bills, for example). These bonds mature in five years and presently pay 6% *at maturity*. If you cash in your series E bonds prior to the five year maturity period, your earnings are *less* than 6% a year! In fact, if you cash in the bonds in the first year, you only make 4.5% interest. In addition, earnings are taxed by federal income tax (though not by state or local taxes).

Series H bonds are similar, though in higher denominations. They too cannot be transferred, sold, or used as collateral. They can be redeemed after six months' waiting time, though the yield is only 5% the first year. Maturity is in 10 years and the rate of interest at maturity is 6%. Hardly a bargain when you consider all the other safe investments earning 6% or more that are far more liquid.

There are a few advantages to these government bonds, especially for people in a high tax bracket. The interest on the Series E bond doesn't have to be declared until the time the bond matures or is cashed in. Thus, Series E bonds can be viewed as a tax-shelter investment, deferring tax liabilities to later years. Of course, over the past 35 years, the government has never failed to extend the maturity date on the Series E bonds on the due date, so conceivably, if you didn't cash in the bonds until your death, they can be passed on to your heirs without any tax on the accrued tax-deferred income.

TREASURY BILLS AND NOTES

Treasury bills, or T-bills, are short-term federal debt instruments issued for periods of 90 days, 180 days or one year. Initially, they are traded in auctions held weekly for 90-day and 180-day bills and once a month for 12-month notes. Bids for offers to purchase T-bills are made by subscribers (banks, large security dealers, and individual investors). An average interest rate of return is deteremined from all the competitive bids and the average becomes the final price. This final price is often referred to as the "non-competitive bid," which is made by investors who simply wish to purchase T-bills at whatever rate is found through competitive bidding. The minimum investment generally is for the $10,000-face value bills. But the treasury has offered in the recent past $1000-face value T-bills, and may do so again in the future.

You can purchase T-bills directly from the Treasury or from a Federal Reserve bank, but is usually is much easier to go through your local bank or a large securities firm. Banks and securities firms generally charge a small commission to handle the transactions, but your personal bank may do it free as a matter of good will. To purchase T-bills from the Treasury by mail, write to: Treasury Department, Bureau of Public Debt, Room 2134, Washington, D.C. 20226. Your letter must follow by no more than a few days a Treasury announcement of an offering. It should state a purchase of noncompetitive trader, giving maturity date (90 days, 180 days, et cetera), social security number, and address to send the Treasury note or bill.

T-bills are far more liquid than Series E & H government bonds. They can also be used as collateral on a loan. Return in recent years has fluctuated from 4% to 9%. And they can be negotiated at any time without loss of accrued interest.

An indirect, more convenient way to buy T-bills is through money market funds which specialize in treasury bill purchases. Capital Preservation Fund, 459 Hamilton Avenue, Palo Alto, CA 94301 (800-227-8380 toll-free, and 800-982-5844 in California), and Fund for Government Investors, Inc., 1735 "K" Street NW, Washington, D.C. 20006 (202-452-9200) are two funds which restrict their fund purchases to short-term government securities. These mutual funds are no-load, open-ended funds which pass on nearly all the treasury yield to investors (management fees are usually less than .5% of yield). And professional "roll-over" techniques can often be used by the fund's managers which result in a better yield than if you purchased a T-bill outright without commission! Both offer a check-writing privilege.

NOTES

56

NOTES

Chapter Five

USING CREDIT CARDS

Although *hard money* advocates shudder and shake their heads at the widespread use of credit cards, believing we have created a plastic economical monster, no one can question that they are an accepted means of buying and selling goods and services in America and most other lands. No less than 510 million credit cards were held by Americans alone in 1979. The prediction by 1989 is an incredible 600 million cards. Banks, airlines, oil companies, large and small stores, and just about everybody else doing business has jumped upon the credit bankwagon. Since Master Card and Visa are by far the two leading charge cards in the United States, let's discuss some of the ways you can get unexpected benefits from these two leading cards.

BORROWING MONEY USING CREDIT CARDS

In recent years, Visa and Master Card have begun offering cash or loan advances through the use of special credit card checks. If you have a Visa or Master Card, you may already have received a number of these special checks along with your monthly statement. These Master Checks or Multipurpose Checks are not the same as regular bank checks. When you use one of these special checks, instead of being charged to your regular checking account, it will be charged to your credit card account and will appear on your monthly billing. Now, perhaps you begin to see the unique opportunity. The benefits of these credit card checks are quite similar to those already mentioned regarding overdraft checking accounts. They amount to nothing less than a personal loan whenever you need one. If used at the start of a new billing period, you will receive 30-35 days before billing begins, and your credit card center will usually ask that you repay 1/20th of the loan advance per month. You can also benefit from *mix payments* in combining special credit card loans with overdraft checking. This is done by writing a personal check to the credit card company to pay off the loan advance. This is then followed up by writing another credit cash advance check to cover the personal check. Due to the float of 2 to 5 days, the personal check will reach the credit card center *before* the cash advance check does, allowing you to "roll over the loan" for another month. Another easy method to "roll over the loan" is to use your cash advance checks with your overdraft checking account, by paying the credit card billing with your overdraft checking account. You then get charged on your overdraft account for the amount of the loan advance. Then, when the overdraft bill comes by mail, you pay off the overdraft account with another cash advance check from Master Card, Visa, or any other credit card offering special checking. You are simply shifting you loan liability from one account to the other.

BORROWING AT LOW INTEREST RATES

Credit cards that offer advance checks allow us to borrow money at far below normal interest rates. Among the ways we can capitalize are: *Flat Fee Programs*; those VISA and Master Card centers that charge a flat fee of 1% (or higher interest) automatically charge for the advance check. If you write a $1000 check, you are charged $10 (or more) for the privilege. There is no additional charge on the cash advance until after the closing date. If you pay off the cash advance in full before the closing date, you will be charged only the flat fee—$10.00 If you decide to finance the loan advance, you'll be billed an additional finance fee on the outstanding balance.

Here's a neat way to reduce effective charges from, let's say 12% a year to as low as a 5% annual rate. First of all, write out the cash advance check a few days before the closing date. By doing this you will have a full two months use of the cash loan (in place of one month) before you'll have to repay the loan. By the time your check clears and is deposited by the credit card center, the closing date will have passed and you can't be billed for the cash advance check until the next month's billing date. The bill you will receive this month has already been prepared. Now, two months later, you'll have to pay back the cash advance loan or be charge more interest. You therefore write out a personal check for the amount of the cash advance and mail it to your credit card center a couple of days prior to the closing date. At this same time, you deposit another cash advance check in your regular checking account to cover your personal check. By the time the card center gets your new cash check, the closing date has passed again, and you have another two months use of the loan at the low 1% or just slightly higher fee.

If you use this method for a full year (12 months) you will only pay a 1% fee six times a year. That's just 6% interest per year. Moreover, you can cut the interest rate even further if you completely pay off the loan advance every other month with an interest-paying checking account. You cover the personal check you send to pay off the credit card bill by depositing your next cash advance check in an interest-paying checking account. During the time it takes for the personal check to clear the bank, you earn some interest on the cash advance.

Daily interest charges. More banks and charge card companies are offering daily interest charge systems for overdraft accounts and cash advances. The rate is usually 12% to 18% per year. You can reduce the interest on your daily interest system: pay the full amount of the cash advance as soon as you receive your credit card billing. Don't wait until a couple of days prior to the closing date. By "rolling over the loan" each month using an interest-paying checking account, you can easily reduce the rate below 10% (on a normal 12% daily interest program), depending on how long it takes for your check to clear.

Interest Free Loans. Banks and savings and loan associations that grant free loans to established clients on a very short term (usually 3 days or less) are few and far between in the good 'ol U.S.A., but if you search long and hard you might find one. In addition to being *scarce as hen's teeth,* they usually restrict their loans to modest amounts. Often one thousand dollars or less.

NOTES

NOTES

Chapter Six

BUSINESS BANKING AND BORROWING

Some small businesspersons cannot understand why a lending institution refuses to lend them money. Others have no trouble getting funds, but they are surprised to find strings attached to their loans. Such owner-managers fail to realize that banks and other lenders have to operate by certain principles just as do other types of business.

This section discusses the following fundamentals of borrowing: (1) credit worthiness, (2) kinds of loans, (3) amount of money needed, (4) collateral, (5) loan restrictions and limitations, (6) the loan application, and (7) standards which the lender uses to evaluate the application.

If you're an investor or budding entrepeneur who needs capital to take advantage of a super investment or great business opportunity, you must learn the art of productive borrowing procedures. Your success or failure may hang in the balance.

Inexperience with borrowing procedures often creates resentment and bitterness. The stories of three small businesspersons illustrate this point.

"I'll never trade here again" William Smith said when his bank refused to grant him a loan. "I'd like to let you have it, William" the banker said, "but your firm isn't earning enough to meet your current obligations." Mr Smith was unaware of a vital financial fact, namely, that lending institutions have to be certain that the borrower's business can repay the loan.

Tom Jones lost his temper when the bank refused him a loan because he did not know what kind or how much money he needed. "We hesitate to lend," the banker said, "to business owners with such vague ideas of what and how much they need."

John William's case was somewhat different. He didn't explode until after he got the loan. When the papers were ready to sign, he realized that the loan agreement put certain limitations on his business activities. "You can't dictate to me," he said and walked out of the bank. What he didn't realize was that the limitations were for his good as well as for the bank's protection.

Knowledge of the financial facts of business life could have saved all three men the embarrassment of losing their tempers. Even more important, such information would have helped them to borrow money at a time when their businesses needed it badly.

This section is designed to give the highlights of what is involved in sound business borrowing. It should be helpful to those who have had little or no experience with borrowing. More experienced owner-managers should find it useful in reevaluating their borrowing operations.

HOW ABOUT CREDIT

The ability to obtain money when you need it is as necessary to the operation of your business as is a good location or the right equipment, reliable source of supplies and materials, or an adequate labor force. Before a bank or any other lending agency will lend you money, the loan officer must feel satisfied with the answers to the five following questions.

1. What sort of person are you, the prospective borrower? By all odds, the character of the borrower comes first. Next is his ability to manage his business.

2. What are you going to do with the money? The answer to this question will determine the type of loan—short or long-term. Money to be used for the purchase of seasonal inventory will require quicker repayment than money used to buy fixed assets. Here, too, it is very important that you make a great presentation, showing that you have planned carefully just how to use borrowed money.

3. When and how do you plan to pay it back? Your banker's judgment as to your business ability and the type of loan will be a deciding factor in the answer to this question.

4. Is the cushion in the loan large enough? In other words, does the amount requested make suitable allowance for unexpected developments? The banker decides this question on the basis of your financial statement which sets forth the condition of your business and/or on the collateral pledge.

5. What is the outlook for business in general and for your business particularly?

It is much easier to get a business loan in a *bullish* economical climate than one that has turned *bearish*. Even if the business climate is sunny and hot, the lending officer must be impressed with your particular enterprise or he will give you a cold shoulder. A strong presentation that is comprehensive and well thought out, is often the deciding factor. Take extra time to prepare a dynamite presentation and you're halfway there to getting money you need.

ADEQUATE FINANCIAL DATA IS A "MUST"

The banker wants to make loans to businesses which are solvent, profitable, and growing. The two basic financial statements he uses to determine those conditions are the balance sheet and profit-and-loss statement. The former is the major yardstick for solvency and the latter for profits. A continous series of these two statements over a period of time is the principal device for measuring financial stability and growth potential.

If you're *selling ideas* and don't have a proven track record, as is the case with a brand new enterprise, the need for a great demonstration of potential profits is absolutely essential. Thank God, there are still lending institutions (although in the minority) who will risk their money on potentially great ideas for new business or investments.

In interviewing loan applicants and in studying their records, the banker is especially interested in the following facts and figures.

Are the books and records up to date and in good condition? What is the condition of accounts payable? Of notes payable? What are the salaries of the owner-manager and other company officers? Are all taxes being paid currently? What is the order backlog? What is the number of employees? What is the insurance coverage?

Are there indications that some of the accounts receivable

have already been pledged to another creditor? What is the accounts receivable turnover? Is the accounts receivable total weakened because many customers are far behind in their payments? Has a large enough reserve been set up to cover doubtful accounts? How much do the largest accounts owe and what percentage of your total accounts does this amount represent?

Is merchandise in good shape or will it have to be marked down? How much raw material is on hand? How much work is in process? How much of the inventory is finished goods?

Is there any obsolete inventory? Has an excessive amount of inventory been consigned to customers? Is inventory turnover in line with the turnover for other businessess in the same industry? Or is money being tied up too long in inventory?

In business loans, lenders also want to know what the type, age, and condition of the equipment is. What are the depreciation policies? What are the details of mortgages or conditional sales contract? What are the future acquisition plans?

WHAT KIND OF MONEY?

When you set out to borrow money for your firm, it is important to know the kind of money you need from a bank or other lending institution. There are three kinds of money: short-term, long-term and equity capital.

Keep in mind that the purpose for which the funds are to be used is an important factor in deciding the kind of money needed. But even so, deciding what kind of money to use is not always easy. It is sometimes complicated by the fact that you may be using some of various kinds of money at the same time and for identical purposes.

Keep in mind that a very important distinction between the types of money is the source of repayment. Generally, short-term loans are repaid from the liquidation of current assets which they have financed. Long-term loans are usually repaid from earnings.

SHORT-TERM BANK NOTES

You can use short-term bank loans for purposes such as financing accounts receivable for, say, 30 to 60 days. Or you can use them for purposes that take longer to pay off—such as for building a seasonal inventory over a period of 5 to 6 months. Usually, lenders expect short-term loans to be repaid after their purposes have been served: for example, accounts receivable loans, when the outstanding accounts have been paid by the borrower's customers, and inventory loans, when the inventory has been converted into saleable merchandise.

Banks grant such money either on your general credit reputation with an unsecured loan or on a secured loan—against collateral.

The *unsecured loan* is the most frequently used form of bank credit for short-term purposes. You do not have to put up collateral because the bank relies on your credit reputation.

The *secured loan* involves a pledge of some or all of your assets. The bank requires security as a protection for its depositors against the risks that are involved even in business situations where the chances of success are good.

TERM BORROWING

Term borrowing provides money you plan to pay back over a fairly long time. Some people break it down into two forms: (1) intermediate—loans longer than 1 year but less than 5 years, and (2) long-term—loans for more than 5 years.

However, for your purpose of matching the kind of money to the needs of your company, think of term borrowing as a kind of money which you probably will pay back in periodic installments from earnings.

EQUITY CAPITAL

Some people confuse term borrowing and equity (or investment) capital. Yet there is a big difference. You don't have to repay equity money. It is money you get by selling a part interest in your business.

You take people into your company who are willing to risk their money in it. They are interested in potential income rather than in an immediate return on their investment.

HOW MUCH MONEY

The amount of money you need to borrow depends on the purpose for which you need funds. Figuring the amount of money required for business construction, conversion, or expansion—term loans or equity capital—is relatively easy. Equipment manufacturers, architects, and builders will readily supply you with cost estimates. On the other hand, the amount of working capital you need depends upon the type of business you're in. While rule-of-thumb ratios may be helpful as a starting point, a detailed projection of sources and uses of funds over some future period of time—usually for 12 months—is a better approach. In this way, the characteristics of the particular situation can be taken into account. Such a projection is developed through the combination of a predicted budget and a cash forecast.

The budget is based on recent operating experience plus your best judgment of performance during the coming period. The cash forecast is your estimate of cash receipts and disbursements during the budget period. Thus, the budget and the cash forecast together represent your plan for meeting your working capital requirements.

To plan your working capital requirements, it is important to know the "cash flow" which your business will generate. This involves simply a consideration of all elements of cash receipts and disbursements at the time they occur. These elements are listed in the profit-and-loss statement which has been adapted to show cash flow (following). They should be projected for each month.

WHAT KIND OF COLLATERAL?

Sometimes, your signature is the only security the bank needs when making a loan. At other times, the bank requires additional assurance that the money will be repaid. The kind and amount of security depends on the bank and on the borrower's situation.

If the loan required cannot be justified by the borrower's

financial statements alone, a pledge of security may bridge the gap. The types of security are: endorsers, comakers, and guarantors; assignment of leases; trust receipts and floor planning; chattel mortgages; real estate; accounts receivable; savings accounts; life insurance policies; and stocks and bonds. In a substantial number of States where the Uniform Commercial Code has been enacted, paperwork for recording loan transactions will be greatly simplified.

ENDORSERS, CO-MAKERS, AND GUARANTORS

Borrowers often get other people to sign a note in order to bolster their own credit. These *endorsers* are contingently liable for the note they sign. If the borrower fails to pay up, the bank expects the endorser to make the note good. Sometimes, the endorser may be asked to pledge assets or securities that he owns.

A *co-maker* is one who creates an obligation jointly with the borrower. In such cases, the bank can collect directly from either the maker or the co-maker.

A *guarantor* is one who guarantees the payment of a note by signing a guaranty commitment. Both private and government lenders often require guarantees from officers of corporations in order to assure continuity of effective management. Sometimes, a manufacturer will act as guarantor for one of his customers.

ASSIGNMENT OF LEASES

The assigned lease as security is similar to the guarantee. It is used, for example, in some franchise situations.

The bank lends the money on a building and takes a mortgage. Then the lease, which the dealer and the parent franchise company work out, is assigned so that the bank automatically receives the rent payments. In this manner, the bank is guaranteed repayment of the loan.

WAREHOUSE RECEIPTS

Banks also take commodities as security by lending money on a warehouse receipt. Such receipt is usually delivered directly to the bank and shows that the merchandise used as security either has been placed in a public warehouse or has been left on your premises under the control of one of your employees who is bonded (as in field warehousing). Such loans are generally made on staple or standard merchandise which can be readily marketed. The typical warehouse receipt loan is for a percentage of the estimated value of the goods used as security.

TRUST RECEIPTS AND FLOOR PLANNING

Merchandise, such as automobiles, appliances, and boats, has to be displayed to be sold. The only way many small marketers can afford such displays is by borrowing money. Such loans are often secured by a note and a trust receipt.

This trust receipt is the legal paper for floor planning. It is used for serial-numbered merchandise. When you sign one, you (1) acknowledge receipt of the merchandise, (2) agree to keep the merchandise in trust for the bank, and (3) promise to pay the bank as you sell the goods.

CHATTEL MORTGAGES

If you buy equipment such as a cash register or a delivery truck, you may want to get a chattel mortgage loan. You give the bank a lien on the equipment you are buying.

The bank also evaluates the present and future market value of the equipment being used to secure the loan. How rapidly will it depreciate? Does the borrower have the necessary fire, theft, property damage, and public liability insurance on the equipment? The banker has to be sure that the borrower protects the equipment.

REAL ESTATE

Real estate is another form of collateral for long-term loans. When taking a real estate mortgage, the bank finds out: (1) the location of the real estate, (2) its physical condition, (3) its foreclosure value, and (4) the amount of insurance carried on the property.

If you own business or residential real estate you have one of the best and fastest methods to obtain loans. The equity in your own family dwelling could allow you to launch a new business or take advantage of an investment opportunity.

ACCOUNTS RECEIVABLE

Many banks lend money on accounts receivable. In effect you are counting on your customers to pay your note.

The bank may take accounts receivable on a notification or a nonnotification plan. Under the *notification* plan, the purchaser of the goods is informed by the bank that his account has been assigned to it and he is asked to pay the bank. Under the *nonnotification* plan, the borrower's customers continue to pay him the sums due on their accounts and he pays the bank.

SAVINGS ACCOUNTS

Sometimes, you might get a loan by assigning to the bank a savings account. In such cases, the bank gets an assignment from you and keeps your passbook. If you assign an account in another bank as collateral, the lending bank asks the other bank to mark its records to show the account is held as collateral.

Using your savings account to nail down a business or investment loan is a perfect example of that old axiom, "You gotta prove to a banker that you don't need the money before he will grant you the loan."

LIFE INSURANCE

Another kind of collateral is life insurance. Banks will lend up to the cash value of a life insurance policy. You have to assign the policy to the bank.

If the policy is on the life of an executive of a small corporation, corporate resolutions must be made authorizing the assignment. Most insurance companies allow you to sign the policy back to the original beneficiary when the assignment to the bank ends.

Some people like to use life insurance as collateral rather than borrow directly from insurance companies. One reason is that a bank loan is often more convenient to obtain and sometimes may be obtained at a lower interest rate.

STOCKS AND BONDS

If you use stocks and bonds as collateral, they must be marketable. As a protection against market declines and possible expenses of liquidation, banks usually lend no more than 75 percent of the market value of high grade stock. On Federal government or municipal bonds, they may be willing to lend 90 percent or more of their market value.

The bank may ask the borrower for additional security or payment whenever the market value of the stocks or bonds drops below the bank's required margin.

WHAT ARE THE LENDER'S RULES?

Lending institutions are not just interested in loan payments. They are also interested in borrowers with healthy profit-making businesses. Therefore, whether or not collateral is required for a loan, they set loan limitations and restrictions to protect themselves against unnecessary risk and at the same time against poor management practices by their borrowers. Often some owner-managers consider loan limitations a burden.

Yet others feel that such limitations also offer an opportunity for improving their management techniques.

Especially in making long-term loans, the borrower as well as the lender should be thinking of: (1) the net earning power of the borrowing company, (2) the capability of its management, (3) the long range prospects of the company, and (4) the long range prospects of the industry of which the company is a part. Such factors often mean that limitations increase as the duration of the loan increases.

WHAT KINDS OF LIMITATIONS?

The kinds of limitations, which an owner-manager finds set upon the company depends, to a great extent, on the company. If the company is a good risk, only minimum limitations need be set. A poor risk, of course, is different. Its limitations should be greater than those of a stronger company.

Look now for a few moments at the kinds of limitations and restrictions which the lender may set. Knowing what they are can help you see how they affect your operations.

The limitations which you will usually run into when you borrow money are:

(1) Repayment terms.

(2) Pledging or the use of security.

(3) Periodic reporting.

A loan agreement, as you may already know, is a tailor-made document covering, or referring to, all the terms and conditions of the loan. With it, the lender does two things: (1) protects his position as a creditor (he wants to keep that position in as well a protected state as it was on the date the loan was made) and (2) assures himself of repayment according to the business terms.

The lender reasons that the borrower's business should *generate enough funds* to repay the loan while taking care of other needs. He considers that cash inflow should be great enough to do this without hurting the working capital of the borrower.

COVENANTS—NEGATIVE AND POSITIVE

The actual restrictions in a loan agreement come under a section known as covenants. Negative covenants are things which the borrower may not do without prior approval from the lender. Some examples are: further additions to the borrower's total debt, nonpledge to others of the borrower's assets, and issuance of dividends in excess of the terms of the loan agreement.

On the other hand, positive covenants spell out things which the borrower must do. Some examples are: (1) maintenance of a minimum net working capital, (2) carrying of adequate insurance, (3) repaying the loan according to the terms of the agreement, and (4) supplying the lender with financial statements and reports.

Overall, however, loan agreements may be amended from time to time and exceptions made. Certain provisions may be waived from one year to the next with the consent of the lender.

YOU CAN NEGOTIATE

Next time you go to borrow money, thrash out the lending

terms before you sign. It is good practice no matter how badly you may need the money. Ask to see the papers in advance of the loan closing. Legitimate lenders are glad to cooperate.

Chances are that the lender may "give" some of the terms. Keep in mind also, that while you're mulling over the terms, you may want to get the advice of your associates and outside advisors. In short, try to get terms which you know your company can live with. Remember, however, that once the terms have been agreed upon and the loan is made (or authorized as in the case of SBA, you are bound by them.

THE LOAN APPLICATION

Now you have read about the various aspects of the lending process and are ready to apply for a loan. Banks and other private lending institutions, as well as the Small Business Administration, require a loan application on which you list certain information about your business.

For purposes of explaining a loan application, the section uses the Small Business Administration's application for a loan (SBA Form 4). The SBA form is more detailed than most bank forms. The bank has the advantage of prior knowledge of the applicant and his activities. Since SBA does not have such knowledge, its form is more detailed. Moreover, the longer maturities of SBA loans ordinarily will necessitate more knowledge about the applicant.

Before you get to the point of filling out a loan application, you should have talked with an SBA representative, or perhaps your accountant or banker, to make sure that your business is eligible for an SBA loan. Because of public policy,

SBA cannot make certain types of loans. Nor can it make loans under certain conditions. For example, if you can get a loan on reasonable terms from a bank, SBA cannot lend you money. The owner-manager is also not eligible for an SBA loan if he can get funds by selling assets which his company does not need in order to grow.

When the SBA representative gives you a loan application, you will notice that most of its sections ("Application for Loan"—SBA Form 4) are self-explanatory. However, some applicants have trouble with certain sections because they do not know where to go to get the necessary information.

Section3—"Collateral Offered" is an example. A company's books should show the net value of assets such as business real estate and business machinery and equipment. "Net" means what you paid for such assets less depreciation.

If an owner-manager's records do not contain detailed information on business collateral, such as real estate and machinery and equipment, he sometimes can get it from his Federal income tax returns. Reviewing the depreciation which he has taken for tax purposes on such collateral can be helpful in arriving at the value of these assets.

If you are a good manager, you should have your books balanced monthly. However, some businesses prepare balance sheets less regularly. In filling out your "Balance Sheet as of _____, 19 _____, Fiscal Year Ends _____," remember that you must show the condition of your business within 60 days of the date on your loan application. It is best to get expert advice when working up such vital information. Your accountant or banker will be able to help you.

Again, if your records do not show the details necessary for working up profit and loss statements, your Federal income tax returns (Schedule C of Form 1040, if your business is a sole proprietorship or a partnership) may be useful in getting together facts for the SBA loan application.

INSURANCE AND PERSONAL FINANCES

SBA also needs information about the kinds of insurance a company carries. The owner-manager gives these facts by listing various insurance policies. If you place all your insurance with one agent or broker, you can get this information from him.

SBA also must know something about the personal financial condition of the applicant. Among the types of information are: personal cash position; source of income including salary and personal investments; stocks, bonds, real estate, and other property owned in the applicant's own name; personal debts including installment credit payment, life insurance premiums, and so forth.

EVALUATING THE APPLICATION

Once you have supplied the necessary information, the next step in the borrowing process is the evaluation of your application. Whether the processing officer is in a bank or in SBA, he considers the same kinds of things when determining whether to grant or refuse the loan. The SBA loan processor looks for:

(1) The borrower's debt paying record to suppliers, banks, home mortgage holders, and other creditors.

(2) The ratio of the borrower's debt to his net worth.

(3) The past earnings of the company.

(4) The value and condition of the collateral which the borrower offers for security.

The SBA loan processor also looks for (1) the borrower's management ability, (2) the borrower's character, and (3) the future prospects of the borrower's business.

NOTES

NOTES

Chapter Seven

HOW TO APPLY FOR A LOAN FROM THE SMALL BUSINESS ADMINISTRATION

Small Business Administration business loans have helped thousands of small firms get started, expand, grow and prosper.

Small manufacturers, wholesalers, retailers, service concerns, farmers and other businesses may borrow from the Agency to construct, expand, or convert facilities, purchase buildings, equipment, materials or obtain working capital.

By law, the Agency may not make a loan if a business can obtain funds from a bank or other private source. You, therefore, must first seek private financing before applying to SBA. This means that you must apply to your local bank or other lending institution for a loan. If you live in a large city —one with more than 200,000 people—you must apply to two banks before applying for a direct SBA loan.

Applicants for loans must agree to comply with SBA regulations that there will be no discrimination in employment or services to the public, based on race, color, religion, national origin, sex or marital status.

SBA, by the direction of Congress, has as its primary goal the preservation of free, competitive enterprise in order to strengthen the Nation's economy.

SBA's specific lending objectives are to *(1) stimulate small business in deprived areas (2) promote minority enterprise opportunity and (3) promote small business contribution to economic growth.*

WHAT IS A SMALL BUSINESS?

For business loan purposes, SBA defines a small business as one that is independently owned and operated, not dominant in its field and meets employment or sales standards developed by the Agency. For most industries, these standards are as follows:

Manufacturing—Number of employees may range up to 1,500, depending on the industry in which the applicant is primarily engaged.

Wholesaling—small if yearly sales are not over $9.5 to $22 million, depending on the industry.

Services—Annual receipts not exceeding $2 million to $8 million depending on the industry in which the applicant is primarily engaged.

Retailing—small if annual sales or receipts are not over $2 to $7.5 million, depending on the industry.

Construction—General construction: average annual receipts not exceeding $9.5 million for three most recently completed fiscal years. Special trade contruction: average annual receipts not exceeding $1 or $2 million for three most recently completed fiscal years, depending on the industry.

Agriculture—Annual receipts not exceeding $1,000,000.

Ask the nearest SBA field office which standard applies to your type of business.

It should already be apparent to you that the Small Business Administration considers some pretty good sized businesses to be *small business*. One of the major criticisms of the SBA is that they do not do enough to help the really small business folks—the mom and pop operators or the entrepreneur who is rich in ideas but poor in start-up capital. We can only hope they will become more active in assisting *shoestring capitalists* in the future.

GENERAL CREDIT REQUIREMENTS

A loan applicant must:

- Be a good character.

- Show ability to operate his business successfully.

- Have enough capital in an existing firm so that, with an SBA loan, he can operate on a sound financial basis.

- Show the proposed loan is of such sound value or so secured as reasonably to assure repayment.

- Show that the past earnings record and future prospects of the firm indicate ability to repay the loan and other fixed debt, if any, out of profits.

- Be able to provide from his own resources sufficient funds to have a reasonable amount at stake to withstand possible losses, particularly during the early stages, if the venture is a new business.

AMOUNTS AND TERMS OF LOANS

SBA emphasizes maximum private lender participation in each loan. This policy has made it possible for SBA to respond to a far greater number of requests for financial assistance than is possible under the direct lending program.

When the financing is not otherwise available on reasonable terms, SBA may guarantee up to 90 percent or $350,000 (or $500,000 in special situations), whichever is less, of a bank loan to a small firm.

If the loan is not obtainable from a private lender and if an SBA guaranteed loan is not available, SBA will then consider advancing funds on an immediate participation basis with a bank. SBA will consider making a direct loan only when these other forms of financing are not obtainable and funds are available for direct lending.

The Agency's share of an immediate participation loan may not, at the present time, exceed $150,000. Direct loans may not exceed $150,000 and at times may not be available due to Federal fiscal restraints. In exceptional circumstances, if certain standards are met, these ceilings may be waived by Regional Directors.

MATURITY

SBA business loans may be for as long as ten years, except those portions of loans for the purpose of acquiring real property or constructing facilities may have a maturity of 20 years. However, working capital loans usually are limited to six years.

INTEREST

Interest rates on SBA's portion of immediate participations, as well as direct loans may not exceed a rate set by a statutory formula relating to the cost of money to the Government (usually between 6% and 7%). Within certain limitations bank sets the interest rate on guaranteed loans and its portion of immediate participation loans.

COLLATERAL

Security for a loan may consist of one or more of these:

• A mortgage on land, a building and/or equipment.

• Assignment of warehouse receipts for marketable merchandise.

• A mortgage on chattels.

• Guarantees or personal endorsements, and in some instances, assignment of current receivables.

A pledge or mortgage on inventories usually is not satisfactory collateral, unless the inventories are stored in a bonded or otherwise acceptable warehouse.

INELIGIBLE APPLICATIONS

Because it is a public agency lending taxpayers' funds, SBA

has an unusual responsibility as a lender. It therefore will not make loans:

- If the funds are otherwise available on reasonable terms.

- If the loan is to (a) *pay off a loan to a creditor or creditors of the applicant who are inadequately secured and in a position to sustain loss;* (b) *provide funds for distribution or payment to the principals of the applicant, or* (c) *replenish funds previously used for such purposes.*

- If the loan allows speculation in any kind of property.

- If the applicant is a nonprofit enterprise.

- If the applicant is a newspaper, magazine, book publishing company, or similar enterprise, except radio, cable, or TV broadcasting companies.

- If any of the gross income of the applicant (or any of its principal owners) is derived from gambling activities, except for those small firms which obtain less than one-third of their income from the sale of state lottery tickets under a state license, or from gambling activities in those states where such activities are legal within the State.

- If the loan provides funds to an enterprise primarily engaged in lending or investing.

- If the loan finances real property that is, or is to be, held for investment.

- If the loan encourages monopoly or is inconsistent with the accepted standards of the American system of free competitive enterprise.

- If the loan is used to relocate a business for other than sound business purposes.

RECREATIONAL ENTERPRISES AND
AND CHANGE OF OWNERSHIP

Amusement and recreational enterprises are eligible for SBA assistance. However, they must be open to the public and properly licensed by appropriate State or local authority.

Loans may be approved to effect a change in the ownership of a business if they would aid in the development of a small business, keep it in operation, and/or contribute to a well-balanced national economy by facilitating ownership of small business concerns by persons whose participation in the free enterprise system has been hampered or prevented because of economic, physical, or social disadvantages, or disadvantages in business or resident locations.

STEP-BY-STEP LOAN PROCEDURES

If, after carefully reading the first part of this chapter, you are not sure of your eligibility or about meeting SBA's objectives, credit, or policy criteria, call or write the nearest SBA office for clarification.

If you believe you qualify and wish to apply for an SBA loan, follow this step-by-step procedure:

FOR ESTABLISHED BUSINESSES

Prepare a current financial statement (balance sheet) listing all assets and all liabilities of the business—do not include personal items.

Have an earnings (profit and loss) statement for the previous full year and for the current period to the date of the balance sheet.

Prepare a current personal financial statement of the owner, or each partner or stockholder owning 20% or more of the corporate stock in the business.

List collateral to be offered as security for the loan, with your estimate of the present market value of each item.

State amount of loan requested and explain exact purposes for which it will be used.

Take this material with you and see your banker. Ask for a direct bank loan and if declined, ask the bank to make the loan under SBA's Loan Guaranty Plan or to participate with SBA in a loan. If the bank is interested in an SBA guaranty or participation loan, ask the banker to contact SBA for discussion of your application. In most cases of guaranty or participation loans, SBA will deal directly with the bank.

If a guaranty or a participation loan is not available, write or visit the nearest SBA office. SBA has 96 field offices and, in addition, sends loan officers to visit many smaller cities on a regularly scheduled basis or as the need is indicated. To speed matters, make your financial information available when you first write or visit SBA.

SBA FIELD OFFICES
(Alphabetically By City)

Agana, GU
Albany, NY
Albuquerque, NM
Anchorage, AK
Atlanta, GA
Augusta, ME
Baltimore, MD
Biloxi, MS
Birmingham, AL
Boise, ID
Boston, MA
Buffalo, NY
Camden, NJ
Casper, WY
Charleston, WV
Charlotte, NC
Chicago, IL
Cincinnati, OH
Clarksburg, WV
Cleveland, OH
Columbia, SC
Columbus, OH
Concord, NH
Coral Gables, FL
Corpus Christi, TX
Dallas, TX
Denver, CO
Des Moines, IA

Little Rock, AR
Los Angeles, CA
Louisville, KY
Lower Rio Grande
  Valley, TX
Lubbock, TX
Madison, WI
Marquette, MI
Marshall, TX
Melville, NY
Memphis, TN
Milwaukee, WI
Minneapolis, MN
Montpelier, VT
Nashville, TN
Newark, NJ
New Orleans, LA
New York, NY
Oklahoma City, OK
Omaha, NE
Philadelphia, PA
Phoenix, AZ
Pittsburgh, PA
Portland, OR
Providence, RI
Rapid City, SD
Reno, NV
Richmond, VA

Detroit, MI   Rochester, NY
Eau Claire, WI   St. Louis, MO
Elmira, NY   Sacramento, CA
El Paso, TX   Salt Lake City, UT
Fairbanks, AK   San Antonio, TX
Fargo, ND   San Diego, CA
Fresno, CA   San Francisco, CA
Greenville, NC   Seattle, WA
Harrisburg, PA   Shreveport, LA
Hartford, CT   Sioux Falls, SD
Hato Rey, PR   Spokane, WA
Helena, MT   Springfield, IL
Holyoke, MA   St. Thomas, VI
Honolulu, HI   Syracuse, NY
Houston, TX   Tampa, FL
Indianapolis, IN   Washington, DC
Jackson, MS   West Palm Beach, FL
Jacksonville, FL   Wichita, KS
Kansas City, MO   Wilkes-Barre, PA
Knoxville, TN   Wilmington, DE
Las Vegas, NV

FOR NEW BUSINESSES

Describe in detail the type of business to be established.

Describe experience and management capabilities.

Prepare an estimate of how much you or others have to invest in the business and how much you will need to borrow.

Prepare a current financial statement (balance sheet) listing all personal assets and all liabilities.

Prepare a detailed projection of earnings for the first year the business will operate.

List collateral to be offered as security for the loan, indicating your estimate of the present market value of each item.

Take this material with you and see your banker. Ask for a direct loan and if declined, ask the bank to make the loan under SBA's Loan Guaranty Plan or to participate with SBA in a loan. If the bank is interested in an SBA guaranty or participation loan, ask the banker to contact SBA for discussion of your application. In most cases of guaranty or participation loans, SBA will deal directly with the bank.

NOTES

NOTES

97

Chapter Eight

GETTING HELP FROM THE SBA

MANAGEMENT ASSISTANCE

The SBA management assistance programs are keyed to furthering the establishment, growth, and success of small businesses. The need for this assistance is pointed up by failures that occur in the small business community every year.

It is estimated that managerial deficiencies cause 9 out of 10 business failures. This represents a tremendous loss to the nation's economy. Many of these business failures probably could have been avoided had the owners received management assistance in time.

A major objective of the SBA is to remedy this situation. Through the facilities of the Office of Management Assistance, SBA works to improve and strengthen the management capabilities of small business men and women.

This section briefly describes various SBA management assistance services. For additional information, please call or write the SBA office near you. A Management Assistance Officer will be there to counsel you. A complete listing of SBA field offices can be found at the end of Chapter 7. For the exact address, see the U.S. Small Business Administration in your local telephone directory under United States Government.

Small business owners today must understand and use

modern methods if they expect to compete successfully. More and more, they are becoming aware of this need and are seeking out the information and counsel which will help them improve their management skills and productivity.

SBA identifies management problems, develops alternate solutions, and helps implement and expand business plans through the Management Assistance Officers who staff the Agency's counseling program. In addition to these professionals, SBA relies heavily on national volunteer organizations such as SCORE (Service Corps of Retired Executives) and ACE (Active Corps of Executives) for individual counseling.

Counseling on problems of marketing, accounting, product analysis, production methods, research, and development is given in SBA field offices. Advice and training are also offered at no charge to people considering going into business on their own.

Moreover, SBA constantly urges private sector organizations to serve the small community. An example of such advocacy is the University Business Development Center.

THE SMALL BUSINESS INSTITUTE

SBA's newest management assistance resource is the Small Business Institute (SBI). With the cooperation of faculty, senior, and graduate students of nearly 400 of the nation's leading schools of business, extended personal counseling is being given to small business owners at no charge.

In a few short years, the program has already been of practical assistance to small business and has given valuable "real life" experience to the student-counselors, improved college-community relations, and saved some businesses from almost certain bankruptcy.

Although participation in the SBI Program is primarily for SBA clients (loan recipients and holder of 8(a) contracts) in most localities, business owners who are interested in availing themselves of this service should contact the Management Assistance Officer in their nearest SBA office. He will be able to determine their eligibility.

SCORE
(Service Corps of Retired Executives)

SCORE is an organization of over 6,000 retired business executives—both men and women—who volunteer their services to help small business owners solve their problems. The collective experience of these SCORE volunteers spans the full range of American enterprise.

Assigned SCORE counselors visit the owners in their places of business. Through careful observation, an analysis is made of each business and its problems. On a complex problem, other volunteer experts may be asked to assist. Finally, a plan is offered to correct the trouble and help the owner through the critical period. This service is provided at no cost to the small business owner.

ACE (Active Corps of Executives) augments SCORE's services and keeps management counseling on a continually updated basis. Its members are active executives from all major industries, professional and trade associations, educational institutions, and many of the professions. Over 2,500 ACE members throughout the country volunteer their specialized kinds of expertise, not usually found in every SCORE chapter.

THE CALL CONTRACTING PROGRAM

The Call Contracting (formerly 406) Program provides management and technical assistance to firms and individuals qualifying under Section 7(i) and 7(j) of the Small Business Act, as amended in 1974. It also allows SBA to initiate and maintain this counseling service for small firms as required. The assistance provided ranges from such categories as Junior and Senior Accounting to Complex Engineering and Electronics, according to the specific needs of the individual recipient, and is offered without charge.

The professional consultants who provide this assistance must meet strict standards and are selected through competitive bidding, or careful negotiation. At least one of these contractors is located in each of SBA's ten regions, and some regions have several.

To determine eligibility for the Call Contracting Program, either as a recipient of the counseling assistance, or as a consultant, contact the Management Assistance Officer at your nearest U.S. Small Business Administration office.

INTERNATIONAL TRADE

The SBA works closely with the Department of Commerce, Eximbank, Overseas Private Investment Corp., and other governmental and private agencies to provide small business with assistance and information on export opportunities. The underlying purpose is to increase small business participation in international trade. Increased emphasis is being given to this aspect.

MANAGEMENT TRAINING

To reach the greatest possible number in the small business community, SBA co-sponsors management training with universities, colleges, distributive education units, trade and professional associations, chambers of commerce, and local business organizations. In some communities, management training is also offered over commercial and educational TV stations.

To meet local small business needs, SBA's management training program encompasses four types of training for present and prospective small business owners: courses, conferences, problem clinics, and pre-business workshops.

COURSES AND CONFERENCES

Management courses provide classroom training on a variety of management subjects. Courses may be general survey of 8 to 10 different areas of business management or a series of in-depth sessions on a single subject. Instructors are drawn from teaching staffs of educational institutions or from professionals such as management consultants, bankers, lawyers, accountants, and others who have teaching ability in addition to expertise in a particular subject.

Instructors are selected and paid by the co-sponsoring organizations. The owner-student is usually charged only a nominal fee to cover expenses.

A conference is usually a one-day or one-evening session (though frequently parts of two or three days) for a group of 50 to 100, and it covers a single management subject. A conference normally features speakers, panel discussions, question-and-answer periods, and work sessions.

PROBLEM CLINICS

In a problem clinic, small groups of owner-managers under the guidance of a leader or moderator give intense, in-depth treatment to a single subject.

Much more of the discussion here comes from the participant's own knowledge and experience. SBA and its co-sponsors act as catalysts to bring together people with interest in a common problem, such as expanding marketing areas, crime prevention, or personnel training in specific types of business.

PREBUSINESS WORKSHOPS

Prebusiness workshops are designed for persons who are interested in operating their own business or those who have been in business for a year or less. They may be one-day sessions or a series of evening meetings totalling six to eight hours.

The purpose of the workshops is to help prospective owner-managers make a careful analysis of what is involved in starting and managing a small business. Workshops are designed to deal with the fundamentals of good management applicable to any type of business. They are not intended to provide in-depth training; but, rather, constitute a management orientation and a guide toward preparation by prospective owners before a business is started.

TRAINING MATERIALS

SBA makes available a variety of materials for its co-sponsored management training programs. Some of them are: prebusiness workshop package, instructor's manuals, 16mm sound/color movies, transparencies for overhead projections, and a "Guidebook for Coordinators of Management Training for Small Business." This booklet provides detailed information to help co-sponsors plan, promote, and implement small business management training programs in cooperation with SBA.

UNIVERSITY BUSINESS DEVELOPMENT CENTER

The University Business Development Center (UBDC) is an example of SBA's urging sector organizations to seek new ways to serve the small business community. UBDC is designed to draw together the total resources—including faculty and students—of a university and to make these resources available to new and existing small businesses. Other government agencies which have pertinent campus programs and additional volunteers from the private sector are part of the UBDC program. Although the UBDC started as a pilot program in 1976, if there is a university near you, check your nearest SBA office. There may be a UBDC in your area.

MANAGEMENT PUBLICATIONS

The services of professional management consultants are readily available to big business firms, but are rarely within the means of small business owners.

To help them keep abreast of modern management techniques and maintain efficient management policies, SBA issues about 300 publications on problems of interest to cross-sections of management, and presents facts and figures in brief. readable, non-technical form. Professionals in many business areas contribute their work as a public service to the needs of small firms.

Management assistance publications which are distributed free through SBA offices include the following leaflet series:

- *Management Aids for Small Manufacturers*—a series dealing with functional problems of small plants; it also concentrates on subjects of interest to administrative executives.

- *Small Marketers Aids*—guides for retail, wholesale, and service firms.

- *Small Business Bibliographies*—reference source for individual types of businesses which apply most directly to counseling.

The following series of booklets are for sale at nominal prices from the Superintendent of Documents, U.S. Government Printing Office, Washington, DC 20402:

- *Small Business Management Series*—devoted to more comprehensive discussions of special management problems of small concerns. More than 35 volumes have been published.

- *Starting and Managing Series*—describing problems of starting and managing specific types of small enterprises. Only the first volume, *Starting and Managing a Small Business of Your Own*, does not deal with specific type of business. Representative titles are *Starting and Managing a Snall Shoestore* and *Starting and Managing a Small Drive-In Restaurant.*

Non-series booklets are also available. They discuss management subjects which do not fit into the series categories, such as: *Managing for Profits*, and *Buying and Selling a Small Business.*

NOTES

NOTES

Chapter Nine

FOREIGN BANKING

When most Americans think about savings, they usually only consider their local neighborhood savings and loan association as the place to save their money. That was worked fairly well in the past, but in the wide-open inflation-fueled investment game of the 1980's, it is often smart to learn new ways to earn and save money. There are many valid reasons why you should consider a foreign banking account—among them: real privacy from over-zealous government snoopers, potentially higher profits, and diversification of your funds in the event (God forbid!) of an international political/economic crisis.

Now, let's look at the various foreign countries that will gladly open an account for you. Let's start with our two closest neighbors, CANADA and MEXICO.

THE BENEFITS NORTH OF THE BORDER

Banks in Canada offer interest-paying checking accounts to their "U.S. Dollar Accounts." Interest rates range from 4% to 12%, depending on worldwide (in place of only American) interest rates. Our friends to the north also offer savings accounts in either Canadian or U.S. dollars. The major reason many savers want only a "U.S. dollar account" is to avoid all the hassle and exchange fees due to steady fluctuation between the U.S. and Canadian dollars. Leading Canadian banks offer interest rates comparable to, and in some cases, better than do American savings and loan associations. Taxes are another matter; as a non-resident of Canada you get stuck with a 15% withholding tax on all the interest you earn. (This withholding tax can be deducted from your U.S. taxes, thus reducing the "sting".) The insiders' monetary game north of our border is played with dual Canadian banking accounts, one in U.S. Funds and the other in Canadian dollars. When the Canadian dollar is at a discount, you transfer your U.S. Dollar Account funds to your Canadian Dollar Paying account. When the Canadian dollars bounce back and are selling at a premium, you switch most of your savings to your U.S. dollar account. Since the U.S.-Canadian dollar is constantly in a state of fluctuation, you can grab quick profits by staying on top of these monetary swings. However, even a 1%, 2%, or 3% swing (either direction) in a week or month, while being quite substantial, won't make you big profits unless you are playing with big numbers. A 2% "swing" on $1,000 is only $20.00. If you are playing with, say, $100,000, it's a different game altogether. A 2% "swing" one way or the other could add up to $1,000 easy profits over a short period of time. Again, the game only works if you (a) have hefty sums to play with, and (b) stay on top of this volatile monetary exchange market.

PROFITS SOUTH OF THE BORDER

In Mexico, the investor or saver has a huge choice of in credible financial opportunities. 18½% interest on Mexican bank deposits is easy to come by. While Americans in general, and next-door-neighbor Californians in particular, love to talk about "possible revolutions" and an unstable political climate, the facts do not bear this out. Mexico's social, economic, and political outlook appears much improved since the major peso devaluation of 1976. Inflation is still too high, over 20% in 1979 with predictions of 20% to 25% for

1980-1981. As high as this is, it actually represents about a 50% decrease from 1974-1977 inflation levels in the 30% to 35% range each year. In 1978 the rate dropped slightly below 20% for the first time since 1972, but jumped up a little past 20% in 1979. President Lopez Portillo seems to be making a serious effort to cut government spending.

MEXICO'S BLACK GOLD

Oil is the *numero uno* reason why Mexico can expect a positive trade balance in the years to come. Proven oil reserves are presently 8 billion barrels and "probable" reserves may reach 30 billion or more. Some Mexican officials see Mexican oil reserves rivaling those of Saudi Arabia. While this could be possible, the prediction may have a heavy bias and be highly optimistic. One thing is certain: there is a good deal of "black gold" beneath Mexican soil and this fact should improve Mexico's economic status in the very near future.

Needless to say, the nation which is still very *third-worldish* and agriculture oriented needs a financial shot in the arm. By American standards, over 75% of Mexican citizens can be labeled as "very poor."

The future of Mexican progress is directly related to its politics. The Portillo government has maintained a stable condition. Still, rumors persist of grave discontent, especially with young intellectuals. An emerging "middle class," still in an infant stage, would seem to be this nation's best and only solid foundation for long-range growth and stability.

111

WHAT NEXT FOR THE PESO?

The peso has maintained at a 22.5 pesos per one dollar for some time. Prior to the fall of 1976, the rate was an unrealistic 12.5 pesos for each dollar. If Mexico's rate of inflation continues at levels of 25% or more above the U.S. rate of inflation, a further devaluation is likely. The new boom in oil may reverse this lower value trend and give the peso the strong backing it needs to be competitive on world money markets.

MEXICAN BANK TIME DEPOSITS

You can earn more interest at Mexican savings banks than almost anywhere else in the world...over double U.S. rates! While many continue to question Mexico's stability, the fact is, no Mexican bank has failed in over 40 years. The government does tax the interest earned by foreigners at a 21 percent rate, based on a portion of the gross interest rate. However, you can take a tax credit on your U.S. taxes equal to the tax Mexico withholds. A two year (24 month) peso time deposit will bring a return of 18½% to 34%. The minimum is generally $1,000 and interest is usually paid monthly.

Mexican financial laws guarantee banking secrecy. Not even the IRS is privy to Mexican bank records. As far as the U.S. tax man is concerned, they (the IRS) require that all forms of interest (domestic or foreign-earned) be subject to taxation.

SWISS BANKING

Swiss banks offer unusual checking accounts that many

prudent savers greatly appreciate. The Swiss banks offer accounts that may be denominated into any leading currency in the world—U.S. dollars, French francs, German marks, Swiss francs, etc. While most Swiss banks will not pay interest on these accounts, it is still possible to save money. You can establish an account in Swiss francs, one of the world's most respected "hard currency" that is expected to appreciate in value. At the same time, you can write your checks in dollars. The most unique feature about Swiss checking accounts is they are set up so you can write your checks in francs, dollars, pounds, or other leading currencies.

SAVINGS ACCOUNTS IN SWITZERLAND

The Swiss call their savings accounts "deposit accounts." Here, too, your account can be in dollars or Swiss francs. Interest rates are extremely low, 2% to 3½% a year. Add to that a 35% withholding tax on all earned interest! There are many reasons the Swiss grant such a slim interest return. *Privacy is a major reason for opening a Swiss savings account. The Swiss maintain the world's most secret banking system.* Also, despite low interest, Americans can still earn 20% or more on their savings. Here, again, conversion is the ploy. In recent years the Swiss franc has gone up in value as the dollar declined. In recent history anyone who used dollars to open a Swiss deposit account and turned the dollars into Swiss currency won out, when later the increased Swiss francs were turned back into U.S. dollars. Although it is strictly speculation, it would seem the Swiss franc will continue to rise in value during the early 1980's. Unless American politicians bite the bullet and put inflation under control, we expect the dollar to continue to decline. The Swiss franc deposit account is the world's best, most liquid space in which to hold savings. While the vast majority of Americans would never even consider putting their savings anywhere but an American bank or S & L, there is no question, the Swiss banking system is the world's finest.

A BRIEF REVIEW OF OTHER
FOREIGN BANKING SYSTEMS

While the majority of Americans who choose to do all or at least part of their banking in a foreign land choose Switzerland, Canada, or Mexico as the nation with which they deal, many other European banks are actively soliciting international business. Let's review some.

BANKHAUS DEAK IN AUSTRIA. This is another highly liquid bank and has a past record of fair dealings with Americans. Much like the Swiss system, savings interest rates are very low, at about 2%, but one can invest any leading world currency and have their choice of currencies at withdrawal time.

DUTCH BANKING. Banks in Amsterdam offer numerous services to American investors that they seek. Interest-paying "current" accounts available in U.S. dollars, Swiss francs, German marks, Japanese yen, and other leading currencies. Many Dutch banks are now advertising high-yielding savings accounts for Americans, with up to 14% interest on 24-month time deposits. The time deposits must be in minimum investments of $1,000. Although in every nation but Switzerland, there is no law on the books to prevent a financial institution from revealing information concerning any of its accounts, the Dutch have a solid history of banking secrecy. If one can feel equally "safe" with a Dutch account, the higher interest yields could make it a very attractive alternative to any other system, including the Swiss. Admittedly, the Swiss franc is a stronger currency than the Dutch kroner, but not to a huge degree. Also, inflation in the Netherlands is only a few percentage points above current Swiss inflation.

BRITISH BANKING. In recent years banks in England have been offering high interest rates to attract new customers. Overall, however, British and American banking is quite similar. Also, higher inflationary trends in England are bound to keep as much or more pressure on the pound as the dollar. Add to this fact that Great Britain does not have a long history of banking secrecy, but does have a record of heavy taxation, and this makes it somewhat difficult to make a strong case for one putting his funds in Great Britain.

WORTH CONSIDERING

In conclusion, putting funds in foreign checking or savings accounts can be somewhat risky. Even "hard" currencies such as the Swiss franc and German mark can depreciate in value over short periods of time. The fluctuations in weaker foreign currencies can really blow one's mind. Example: In 1975 the South African rand dropped 18% in one day. In February, 1976, the Spanish peseta dropped 10% in a day, during a 90-day period in 1976 the Italian lira nose-dived 25%. British sterling dropped 5% within two weeks in 1976, and the Mexican peso "floated" downstream 40% on August 31st and September 1st, 1976. Yes, 1976 was a "difficult year" for many of the world currencies. It can, however, happen again and probably will, sometime during the 1980's. Which currencies will be hit the hardest? That's the $64,000 Question. While liking the "hard" aspects of the German mark and Swiss franc best, no currency is absolutely safe. The policy of a nation's financial and political leaders always must determine the ultimate fate of that nation's money.

NOTES

NOTES

Chapter Ten

ALTERNATIVE WAYS TO FIND MONEY

FACTORING

A factor is one who buys business expectancies at rates in direct ratio to the probability of cashing in. In other words, he lends money on odds.

He will advance money against receivable accounts, up to 80% of the invoice amount, and may let the borrower collect his own accounts and turn over the proceeds to him, the factor. He advances money against accounts receivable and may collect himself. He, in effect, buys the account.

He may buy equipment, machinery, land, and buildings, and lease them back.

He may lend money, secured by some asset like merchandise or machinery, for tooling up and buying for a new product or other special purpose. He will lend money on almost any reasonable expectancy, providing he is covered by adequate security or collateral and is repaid with interest, carrying charges, and risk insurance.

Depending on your situation, you can make money with the factor's cash. If you had an opportunity to make a profit by making a certain product in a hurry, you might lose the opportunity if you waited to collect on your accounts receivable. So you borrow against your receivables.

Many banks have entered the factoring field as well as

other loan institutions and insurance companies.

You can borrow against a ready-made market to obtain capital to tool up for making a new product. A factor might lend money to you on your potential sales, or buy and lease back any of your current assets, or lend you money on collateral. You could get a loan against your inventory, especially if the price is going up. Factors have been known to lend money on options, contracts, patents, or prospects if the supporting evidence shows a better than even chance of getting the money back. Of course, the higher the risk, the higher the cost of the money.

Whenever pursuing the factoring angle there are some cautions you should take. Organized crime and crooked elements in some labor unions have set up factoring and small loan operations which bleed the unwary. While they seem to be respectable, you should take the necessary steps to be certain they are by talking with banks, well-known brokers, SBA, police, and any other consumer protection agencies that might know whether or not a business is legitimate.

But don't cross honest and legitimate factors off your lists.

They have lifted thousands of businesses over rough spots and have financed the growth of successful businesses.

Factoring, however, should be used only as a last resort, especially if you have little or no experience with them. Try your banks, SBA, and other outlets first.

SELF FACTORING

Sometimes you may need only small amounts of money for short periods of time and it may not be worth the hassle of applying for a loan. Do-it-yourself factoring may be the answer.

Check out the "clearance house" advertising agency which will clear and pay for your ads in out-of-town newspapers. They will charge you 2% to 6% providing they are only required to do bookkeeping. This will save you from 6% to 15% of the usual agency fees.

When you pay your company bills, you probably pay them within 30 days to keep your company credit rating good. If you missed a payment, it takes from 60 to 90 days before the company you owe will make a black mark on your record and send a collector. This gives you the opportunity to use that extra cash and get ahead on your cash flow, *provided your timing is right*. Many small companies make their payments every 90 days instead of thirty. While you may have to pay a late charge, it may still work to your advantage by the extra sales you could generate with the cash flow.

Perhaps your suppliers are being factored as an account receivable. You know he is probably paying out a lot of money in interest and charges. Offer the supplier to pay 10 days early on your account for 1% or 2% discount. Then work with the supplier to get his other big accounts to do the same thing. This way, the supplier will be able to eliminate his factor and realize a greater profit, while you save some money on supplies.

Suppose your accounts receivable are growing to a point where you are forced to consider factoring in order to meet the demand. Try using a rubber stamp offering your accounts the saving feature of a deduction for discounting bills in 10 days. If enough of the invoices are discounted, your need for a factor can be eliminated.

These tricks of self factoring or avoiding the need for factoring are just a very few. As business people, we are always or should always be looking for ways to cut costs. A reliance on factoring can sometimes be just plain laziness or an unresourcefull approach to the problem at hand. Ask yourself, "Do I want to get rich? Or do I just want to get by?" The answer to that will tell you that you do have the resources to cut costs. All you have to do is look harder.

LEASING

Leasing things today is a way of life. Just about anything you can buy can be leased. Some advantages of leasing are that companies can have use of productive capital equipment while conserving capital for more active turnover on products or expansion. Financial statements can look better to a bank or underwriter without the drain of large capital expenditures. Companies can show a better debt-to-worth ratio in negotiating deals, consolidations, or mergers. Government procurement departments and services will allow equipment rental charges to be added in a cost plus-fixed-fee contract, but disallow interest on money borrowed to buy equipment. Fleets of trucks and autos are services and insured by the lessor, thus saving the lessee the bookkeeping and expenses of servicing and insuring them, as well as the large lump sum purchasing price. Firms that manufacture seasonal or fad items might find it best to lease equipment until the season or fad ends.

When you consider leasing, it is important to do a little arithmetic to determine if leasing is worth it. If you are not realizing a substantial saving in leasing versus buying, then it may be to your advantage to buy the equipment. Remember that the equipment itself can be added to your total equity if you are buying.

If the business you do with leased equipment gives you a net income of less than 10% per year, you certainly can't afford three-year rental contracts. This is true if the equipment rental aggregates more than 30% of the equipment price.

Many rental contracts require a three-year lease agreement. This does not help you if you only need the item for one year. Negotiate a one-year contract or else buy the equipment through a financing agency, and then sell it after you're through with it. In some cases, you might come out a few dollars ahead.

Don't lease equipment that will be used only 50% of the time. You'll lose money. You might find it better to farm out that 50%-of-the-time production.

If the cost of rental, maintenance, and service will cost you over 30% for a long-term contract, you are better off borrowing money to buy the equipment. It will probably cost you less—a lot less if the business is good.

TO LEASE—OR NOT TO LEASE

A good business person takes time to read the newspapers.

Not only do you get a picture on the possible future of your business, you can also spot possible sales outlets. And if you are looking for some equipment, chances are, you may find it in the classified section at a reduced price.

Once a leasing company has made money on its equipment, generally they will recondition it and sell it at less than half the original cost. A reconditioned piece of equipment that sold new at a million dollars may be advertised at "$100,000 or best offer."

A rule of thumb to follow—if you need the equipment for long periods and the lease cost will equal or surpass the actual cost, buy!

TAX ANGLES OF LEASING

You can deduct the cost of leasing. However, you should know what constitutes a lease as far as the IRS is concerned.

According to the Treasury Department, "if a taxpayer acquires the use of business equipment of less than its useful life, with no provision for renewal, such arrangements for Federal income tax purposes constitutes, under the facts, a lease." In other words, if you rent a piece of equipment for one year at smaller payments than would be if you were buying, and the useful life of the equipment might be 3 years, then it is considered a lease. The dividing line here is vague, however, as in most of our tax laws. You should check with IRS or with a sharp tax lawyer. In many cases, a lease agreement may constitute a sales contract for tax purposes.

When everything is considered, a lease may not be as advantageous tax-wise than outright purchase of the equipment. There are circumstances in which a lease can be a great tax advantage.

The tax advantage of leasing should not be the only consideration. If you pay for anything over a period of time instead of all at once, you have the use of money. But you pay for this in the monthly payments. Take care to look at the projected depreciation of the equipment.

Of all the advantages in leasing, don't let them mislead you into a long-term contract for a piece of equipment your company cannot afford.

SALE AND LEASEBACK

One way to raise operating capital is through the sale and lease back of the equipment you have on hand. In effect, you sell your equipment to someone and then lease it back.

This gives you capital to buy supplies or whatever you need to continue your business. This method is a combination of self factoring and leasing. You can negotiate your own lease payments at a level you know you can afford and still use your equipment with the option to buy back at a later date.

There are some dangers to watch out for.

1. Never try to sell and lease back equipment that you don't use very often or try to sell for more than it is worth. You are assuming the buyer is stupid and you may find yourself in a costly lawsuit.

2. Be sure you do not default on your lease back payments. You may find competitors using your own equipment to put you out of business.

3. If you are going to need the equipment a lot longer than the lease agreement, be sure you include an option to buy clause, or a lease renewal clause in the contract. It is assumed you are using the sale and lease back for a program in which you plan to make a profit. It would be to your advantage to include the option to buy clause. Here, your abilities in negotiating come into play. If you are not overly confident in that respect, let your lawyer or business consultant handle the deal.

START YOUR OWN BANK!

No, I'm not kidding! It really is possible for an individual (or group of investors) to get into the banking business. There are real risks involving start-up costs. The process of making a proposal to the Federal Deposit Insurance Corporation (FDIC) in hopes they will grant you a banking charter is costly. You can expect to spend at least FIFTY Thousand Dollars in *legal* and *paperwork* fees before the FDIC even votes to accept or reject a new charter for you and/or your group. Add to this, setting up a board of directors who will have to donate hundreds of hours working on your bank's formation. The three primary criteria for judging a bank's viability are: **Market Area Consideration** *(will you be located in an area that needs another financial institution),* **your proposed executive management team** *(do you have capable men and women to staff a new bank),* and **who will make up your board of directors** *(are these folks well-respected in the community and known for sound judgment)?*

Your sworn answers to these three vital questions will go a long way toward getting your application accepted or rejected.

When an application is submitted, the proposed bank and everyone connected, can expect a rigorous examination of past financial and personal conduct by the regulatory authorities. Within one year a decision is made. If your request is denied, you can reapply at a later date. If an application is approved, you must incorporate within a limited time and seek further approval of your articles and bylaws. You must also obtain FDIC insurance and raise initial capital to run your newly formed bank. It usually takes $1.5 million to $2 million in startup funding. That means you sell stock (usually the board of directors take 25% to 40% of all stock themselves). This usually takes another six months. Only after the completed stock sale and FDIC final approval is your banking charter granted, allowing you to open the doors and do business. The whole process is more than a little risky (you can hit a snag anywhere in the long approval process) and time consuming (generally, it takes 2 to 3 years from conception to "grand opening"). Yet, the rewards are there. Businessmen and entrepreneurs are starting new banks all the time. The high rollers figure the potential rewards are worth the high risk. If they are successful, the sharpies know they have a tailor-made source of investment capital. If you are really interested in going after your own banking charter, you can write the ABA Library, American Banking Association, 1120 Connecticut Avenue NW, Washington, DC 20036, for more details and a list of articles for starting a commercial bank.

NOTES

Chapter Eleven

PRIVACY IN FINANCIAL AFFAIRS

Today, more than at any other time in this nation's history, the long nose of government is constantly "sniffing" around in our financial dealings. This unwanted personal and financial governmental snooping has driven many American investors to seeking private investing and banking in foreign lands.

A regular checking account at an American bank is wide-open to all sorts of government snooping. Uncle Sammy has the right to examine your checking account for any reason he desires. Your checking (or savings) account is anything but private. There is just no way to hide. Your cancelled checks are now put on microfilm and filed for up to twenty years or more. Thus, a record of every bill you ever paid by check or item you purchased has become a permanent record that can quickly be retrieved from various government files. Your cancelled checks become a mirror of your whole financial life.

FIGHTING THE SYSTEM

While it is not easy to beat the snoopers at their own insidious game, here is a plan of action that can stymie their privacy invading tactics:

1. Upon opening a checking account, tell your banker that privacy is important to you. Insist that the bank notify you whenever a third party asks to see your records.

2. By law you need not give your social security number

when you open an account. If you value privacy, you will never give your social security number. For it is this "number" that allows the government to strip you of your precious privacy.

3. Consider using checks that will not reproduce (there is no law against doing so—as yet!). Liberty Graphics, Box 3614, Charlotte, NC 28203, offers checks on dark red paper that will not reproduce well on bank copying film. By using black ink on these dark red checks, it can be almost impossible to reproduce.

MONEY ORDERS

Money orders (from a bank, store, or the post office) can be an effective means of paying bills, making purchases, etc. They are also a very discreet method of transferring funds. You can purchase money orders without giving your name at banks, stores, or the post office. Still, if anyone chooses to keep more detailed records, it likely will be banks. Your corner market or neighborhood liquor store or drug store are your safest privacy bet. Money orders are recorded and filed by the institutions (American Express, various banks, etc.) that issue them. However, they are filed by their number and not by your name. This insures real privacy. The only two big drawbacks to money orders are (a) you must pay a premium to buy them—often 1% to 2% of their value and (b) many stores only offer them in relatively small sums each—such as $200.00 or less, although you can buy as many as your desire.

TRAVELERS CHECKS

Available from many outlets (Bank of America, Travelers

Express, American Express, Thomas Cook, etc.), travelers checks are a great substitute for cash. Much of what I just said about money orders also applies here. They are generally recorded by number and not by the purchaser's name. Nevertheless, most people who seek more freedom in their financial affairs tend to prefer money orders over travelers checks. This, despite the fact that the travelers check is a far more negotiable vehicle in making most "store-bought" purchases.

CASH

Cash is the ultimate method to handle all financial dealings. In using cash, there need be no record whatsoever of the transaction. It is always held in high esteem, and the man or woman who uses it wisely can buy almost anything in the marketplace with it...often at a discount, since many sellers realize the value of "cash payment." On the negative side, rising crime statistics indicate it can be very dangerous to your personal welfare to carry large sums of cash on your person or to have it on hand at your business or home address. If you decide to conduct a large portion of your financial affairs with cash, keep that fact a secret from *all* outside parties.

SEVEN TIPS ON SECURING FINANCIAL PRIVACY

Keep your bank account as confidential as possible.

1. *Become a private investor.*

2. *Use a fictitious company name.*

3. *Use an unlisted telephone number.*

4. *Use a post office box address.*

5. *Borrow money confidentially.*

6. *Use cash, money order, cashier's checks, and travelers checks, whenever possible, for discreet financial dealings.*

7. *Never willing cooperate with any local, state, or federal agency. (By this we mean never volunteer anything to anybody.)*